Revolutionary Soldiers Buried In Illinois

By

MRS. HARRIET J. WALKER

CLEARFIELD

Originally published
Los Angeles, 1917

Reprinted
Genealogical Publishing Company, Inc.
Baltimore, Maryland, 1967

Reprinted for
Clearfield Company, Inc. by
Genealogical Publishing Co., Inc.
Baltimore, Maryland
1992, 1999

Library of Congress Catalogue Card Number 67-28602
International Standard Book Number: 0-8063-0370-0

Made in the United States of America

To the abiding memory of the Soldiers of the Revolution who lie buried in Illinois;

To the Daughters of the American Revolution of Illinois---and to

Mrs. Ella Park Lawrence,

This book is affectionately dedicated.

PREFACE

The perfect history has yet to be written. We cannot trust to myths, legends, or traditions, but must rely upon facts. In the preparation of this work, every effort has been made to obtain the records of these soldiers, to verify them, and to ascertain their places of burial. This has been accomplished in various ways, by ascertaining the names of all who were pensioned and where the application was made. This does not always locate the burial place owing to the changing of the boundary lines of the counties of the state, making it necessary to obtain from the U. S. Treasury department the time and place of payment of the last pension.

Every county history has been studied and many records have thus been established, and burial places located. Valuable information has been obtained from descendants of these soldiers, as well as from aged citizens of the state.

Notwithstanding all the painstaking research, there are many soldiers the exact spot of whose burial will never be known, since in the early days burials were in private burying-grounds which are now fields of grain, then in the old cemeteries owing to lack of marking, the place can only be approximated. The exact place of more than two hundred of these soldiers is known, and over one hundred have been marked by descendants or by patriotic societies.

It is not claimed that these records, either in numbers or in printed report are always entirely authentic. It is a source of regret that it was impossible to visit every one of the eighty-one counties to search the records, and to interview aged citizens, which would have given authenticity to many of the printed records, and doubtless have added many more names of Revolutionary soldiers to the list of heroes. Should other names be obtained, recognition will be made and the additions will be properly preserved.

My most cordial thanks are due to several chapters of the D. A. R. of the state, for assistance in obtaining records and in locating many graves. The kindness of the Hon. Lawrence Y. Sherman, the Hon. James M. Graham, the Hon. T. S. Williams, Col. W. H. Johnson, Prof. George W. Brown, J. N. Gridley and A. T. Strange is appreciated.

Courtesy received at the Newberry Library in Chicago, and the State Historical Library in Springfield, has aided in the preparation of this work.

In an especial manner do I recognize the uniform kindness of the Hon. Pierson W. Banning, vice-president of the Sons of the Revolution of the State of California, whose never-flagging interest in the patriotic thought underlying this historical research has been an inspiration not only in obtaining the addition of nearly one hundred names to the list through access to the valuable reference library of the Sons of the Revolution, in Los Angeles, California, but in the publishing of the book as well.

To Mrs. Ella Park Lawrence, honorary State Regent of the D. A. R. of Illinois, whose patriotic philanthropy has long been recognized in the State as well as the National society, I am personally indebted for making it possible to give to the State of Illinois such an artistic volume on historical research as an addition to the centennial history of the State.

Springfield, Illinois
January—1918

INTRODUCTION

On December 3d, 1918, Illinois will pass the century mark in her history as a member of the galaxy of states in the Union. The general interest in this important anniversary has naturally aroused much original research into the history of the state. Old residents have found in their possession many unpublished documents, dating back to the earliest days in her history, which were fast becoming undecipherable by age and which would have been lost by neglect. From these papers valuable information has been obtained and placed on record in the archives of the state. The few remaining pioneers, too, have recalled and retold priceless stories of the early days, of the growth of the state, educationally, in the religious world, and in the great political crises which have been met in our history. All these will form, in time, the "Folk Lore" of Illinois. Perhaps in no part of research has greater interest arisen than in the study of Illinois in the American Revolution, and in the social and historical development of the fifty or more years following the close of the War for Independence.

Illinois can claim but few spots famous in the era of that war, but around the names of old Fort Massac, Kaskaskia, and Fort Gage, cluster treasured historic memories. Now that Fort Massac has become the property of the State of Illinois and has been transformed into a beautiful State Park, the people of the entire state have justifiable pride in its preservation. To the Daughters of the American Revolution of Illinois, especially, this historic spot is of more than ordinary interest. It was fitting that they should have been actively engaged in erecting a monument there which will ever stand as a memorial of what George Rogers Clark and his soldiers did for Virginia, Illinois, Indiana, Kentucky, and for the Nation. From the lips of many returned soldiers who came with Clark from

Virginia, the people heard of the great Northwest country and decided to emigrate, forming small colonies, and some of these reached the Illinois country as early as 1787, locating in St. Clair and Randolph counties.

Later, word was transmitted to the Eastern states of the attractiveness of the new country, so many more decided to remove to the "Far West." These pioneers were actuated by different motives, the larger number coming because they had heard of the broad rolling prairies and of the forests primeval which would afford greater resources for accumulating a competency than existed in the Eastern country.

With these early settlers came many Revolutionary soldiers. Those who came as early as 1781 and even later, were comparatively young men who had rendered service in the war. They brought their families with them, while in the later immigration were aged men who came with sons or daughters to pass their last days in a strange land where the discouragements incident to a newly settled country might well try the souls of the strongest, and which caused many a homesick feeling as they had left behind the friends of younger days.

Historical research has ascertained that over six hundred came to Illinois—they died and are buried in the state. Eighty-one counties are honored as being the burial places of these men who belonged to the Nation's "Roll of Honor." They came from all the original states and from Vermont and Kentucky. More than five hundred were granted pensions from the Government, while others whose records of service have been established never applied for a pension.

Some have long slept in unmarked graves beneath the roots of tangled weeds of fields or country graveyards; others lie where tottering slabs of slate still mark their last resting place; while a few are honored by stately monuments erected by descendants who treasure the memory of their ancestors.

Bronze markers have been placed in seven counties by the Sons and Daughters of the American Revolution, bearing the names of Revolutionary soldiers buried in the respective counties, and every tablet has been unveiled by lineal descendants of men whose names were engraved in bronze. In addition, Government stones or markers have been placed at the graves of a large number of soldiers buried in the state.

This is at once just and appropriate since we should never forget the brave deeds of these men who helped to establish our government, believing as we do that by performing such duties we intensify the patriotism of our people. It matters not whether the soldier was a Washington, a La Fayette, or one of the "ragged regimentals" of Valley Forge, all are entitled to honor.

This research has covered a period of over six years. It has been a "labor of love," the only reward being the recovery from possible oblivion of the names of these soldiers with their records of service, and so far as possible their burial places, thereby adding an important page to the history of Illinois, which has the distinct honor of being the only state that has undertaken such combined research.

As we call the roll of these pioneer-patriots, whose voices have been silent for more than half a century, there comes no response. It remains, therefore, for us to speak in their behalf, remembering that "The nation that forgets to honor its heroes will soon cease to be heroic."

Adams County

SAMUEL CONNER served in the war from Virginia. He came to Adams county, Illinois, to reside, where he applied for a pension. "Virginia Records."

JOHN COTTON was born in South Carolina in 1753. He enlisted at Camden under Capt. William McClintock, and Col. Thomas Sumpter. He was sergeant of his company, was wounded in the shoulder and was discharged at Augusta, Georgia, three months after the close of the war. He came to Adams county, Illinois, to reside, where he died leaving a large family of children. He was pensioned.

HENRY COVELL was a native of Connecticut. He enlisted at Danbury as a "Minute Man" in April, 1775, serving until December with Capt. Noble Benedict, Col. David Waterbury; he enlisted again in the summer of 1781 for one year and five months under Capt. Solomon Woodworth and Col. Marinus Willett of New York, marched from Fort Plain to German Flats, where on Sept. 7, 1781, their company was all captured or killed by the Indians. Covell, with four others, was carried to Fort Niagara and turned over to the British. He was kept in close confinement until December, 1782, when he was sent to Boston where he was discharged. After the war he removed to New York city, and in 1832 came to Adams county, Illinois, where he died, very aged, about 90 years old. He was pensioned.

JOHN FEE was from Pennsylvania where he served in the war from Washington county. He also remained in the army after the close of the Revolutionary war. He came to Adams county, Illinois, before 1832, and is probably buried there. "Penna. Archives."

STEPHEN JONES was born in New Jersey. He enlisted in Capt. Cornelius Williams' company, 2d regiment, from Essex county. Coming to Illinois, he settled in Adams county in the second ward, where he is probably buried in the city of Quincy. He was pensioned.

JOHN MARTIN served in the war from Virginia. He came to Adams county, Illinois, where he applied for a pension, but not having served six months it was not granted. "Virginia Records."

SAMUEL SHAW was born in Ireland in 1756. Coming to America, he joined the Continental army, enlisting from Cumberland county, Pennsylvania. He served four times, in 1776 for two months with Capt. John Clarke and Col. Frederick Watts, second for four months in 1777 under Capt. David Mitchell; third time for three months in 1778 with Capt. William Blaine and Col. Samuel Lyon, and the fourth time for two months with the same officers. He was in the battles of White Marsh, and Gulf Mills. He came to Adams county, Illinois, and died there July 1, 1853, aged 77 years. He was pensioned.

CHARLES SHEPHERD was a native of Pennsylvania, where he served in the Pennsylvania Artillery, 4th regt. from February, 1777, to November 3, 1783. He removed to New York and from there after 1818 to Adams county, Illinois, settling in Quincy, in the third ward, where he is probably buried. He was pensioned.

DAVID STRAHAN was born in North Carolina March 1, 1755. He served from that state. Coming to Illinois he settled in Adams county, where he died in 1838, and is buried four miles southeast of Clayton in the Baptist cemetery. He was pensioned.

DR. DANIEL WOOD was a native of New York. He served as a surgeon in William Malcom's Additional regiment from March, 1777, to April, 1779, New York troops. His son, John Wood, born in Moravia, N. Y., came to Quincy, Adams county, Illinois, and was elected lieutenant governor of the state in 1856. He served as governor upon the death of Governor Bissell, March 18, 1860. During this time he removed the remains of his father, Dr. Daniel Wood, to Quincy, where he lies buried in Woodland cemetery. "New York in the Revolution, and County History."

Alexander County

GEORGE BROWN was born in Rowan county, North Carolina, in 1755. He enlisted there in the fall of 1776, serving two months under Capt. James Montgomery and Col. Francis Locke. He again enlisted in the summer of 1779, serving five and one-half months under Quartermaster Yarberry. He removed to Tennessee, and from there to Union county, Illinois, but died in Alexander county December 10, 1846. He was pensioned.

ADAM CLAPP served in the war from North Carolina. He came to Union county, Illinois, in 1809, settling on Sandy Creek, which is now in Alexander county, where he probably died. He was on the grand jury in Union county in 1818. He was pensioned.

Bond County

JOHN DIAMOND was from South Carolina, where he served in the war. He came to Illinois in 1820, settling in Fayette county, but died in Bond county and is buried in the Old Diamond cemetery, near Zion Springs. He was pensioned.

PETER HUBBARD was born in 1747 in South Carolina. He served three years under Capt. Samuel Wise and Capt. John Carraway Smith, with Col. William Thompson. He was a lieutenant and was in the battle of Sullivan Island. He removed to Tennessee and from there to Bond county, Illinois, where he died. He was pensioned.

JAMES LONG served from Virginia. Coming to Illinois, he settled in Bond county, where he died and is buried in the Smith graveyard. "Virginia Records."

JOSEPH McADAMS was born in York county, Pennsylvania, in 1759. He enlisted from Hawfield, Orange county, North Carolina, serving under Col. John Armstrong, Col. William O'Neale, and Col. Robert Melone. He was also a pilot under Col. Lee. He was in the battles of Stono, Hillsborough and Holt's Race Paths. He came to Bond county, Illinois, where he died, and is buried six miles south of Greenville, in what is known as the "Camp Ground." He was pensioned.

JACOB NEER was from New York, where he served in the Eighth Albany County Militia under Col. Robert Van Rensselaer. He came to Bond county, Illinois, where he died, and is buried in the Smith graveyard, three miles southwest of Greenville. "New York in the Revolution."

WILLIAMSON PLANT was born in Louisa county, Virginia, in 1763. He early enlisted in the Fifth Regiment, serving under Capt. Richard Clough in the Virginia troops. He again enlisted in the militia, serving at various times until the close of the war. He came to Bond county, Illinois, where he died in 1830, and is buried in the old graveyard in Pocahontas. "Virginia Records."

HEZEKIAH ROWE was born in South Carolina June 17, 1759. He served in the South Carolina troops. He came to Bond county, Illinois, and died there in 1835. He was pensioned.

THOMAS WHITE was from Pennsylvania, where he served as lieutenant in Col. Bull's regiment of flying troops. He was in Capt. William Armstrong's company; was taken prisoner November 16, 1776, and carried to New York, where he endured great suffering. He escaped June 27, 1777, and again enlisted in Col. William Montgomery's regiment. He came to Bond county, Illinois, and died there; is buried near Greenville. "Pennsylvania Archives."

Boone County

THOMAS HART was born March 23, 1757, in Farmington, Conn. He enlisted in 1776 and served one year. Coming to Illinois, he settled in Boone county, where he died December 12, 1845. His grave was marked by the Rockford Chapter, D. A. R. "Connecticut in the Revolution."

TIMOTHY LEWIS was born in Ashfield, Mass., May 24, 1764. He served as a substitute for his father, Timothy Lewis, in April, 1779, in Capt. Eliphalet Densmore's company for six months; he again served under Capt. Isaac Newton in Col. Hugh Maxwell's regiment in 1780. He came to Boone county, Illinois, where he died May 2, 1858. "Massachusetts Soldiers in the Revolution."

ISAIAH WILLIAMS was a native of Vermont, but he served in the war in the third regiment, Dutchess county, New York militia. He came to Boone county, Illinois, and died there. "New York in the Revolution."

Brown County

WILLIAM KENDRICK was born in Virginia, in 1749. He enlisted in 1779 under Capt. Thomas Armisted and Col. John Green, serving eighteen months. He was in the battles of Guildford Court House, Camden and Ninety-six, also Eutaw Springs. He came to Brown county, Illinois, where he died near Mt. Sterling December 29, 1835. He was pensioned.

JOHN SIX (SAXE) enlisted in the Virginia troops when only sixteen years of age, taking the place of his stepfather. He was present at the surrender of Cornwallis. He removed to Pennsylvania, then to Tennessee, and from there to Kentucky, coming to Scott county, Illinois, in 1825. He lived for fifteen years in Pike county, but died at the home of his son in 1848 in Versaille township, Brown county. He was pensioned.

RICHARD STILES was from Massachusetts, where he served in Capt. John Burnham's company and Col. Michael Jackson's regiment. He enlisted November 1, 1777, serving until January 27, 1778. He came to Brown county, Illinois, to reside, where he applied for a pension, but having served less than six months it was not granted. He died in Brown county. "Massachusetts Soldiers and Sailors in the War."

Bureau County

AARON STURGIS was from Connecticut, where he served in the war. He was a musician in Capt. Ozias Marvin's regiment, Fourth Brigade, under Brigadier Gen. Gold Sellick Siliman. He enlisted May 1, 1778, for three years. He came to Bureau county, Illinois, where he died October, 1842. He was pensioned.

Carroll County

DANIEL CHRISTIAN was born in Pennsylvania in 1762. He enlisted at Reading September, 1776, serving two months under Capt. George Willis. He again served for the same length of time with Capt. Kit. He served for the third time for seven months in 1780 under Capt. John Spohn and Col. Thomas Butler. He removed to Maryland, and from there to Mt. Carroll, Carroll county, Illinois, where he died December 26, 1847, and is buried in Mt. Carroll. He was pensioned.

Cass County

COLBAY CREED was born in Orange county, Virginia, May 4, 1758. While residing in Surrey county, North Carolina, he enlisted in Capt. James Giddings' company of militia. He came to Morgan county, Illinois, but died in Cass county. He was pensioned.

PHINEAS UNDERWOOD was born in Vermont in 1763. He enlisted in Capt. Josiah Fish's company, serving ten months. In 1826 he came to Cass county, Illinois, settling near what is now the city of Virginia. He was buried in a neglected graveyard, but in 1912, through the efforts of the Grand Army Post of Virginia, his remains were removed to Walnut Ridge cemetery, where a United States Government marker tells the story of this patriot. "Vermont in the Revolution and Family History."

Champaign County

ROBERT BROMFIELD was born in Pennsylvania June 4, 1760. He served in the Westmoreland county militia. He removed to Kentucky, and from there, in 1833, to Champaign county, Somer township, Illinois, where he died June 17, 1841, and is buried in the Rheinharts cemetery. "Pennsylvania Archives."

WILLIAM HAYS served in the war from Massachusetts in Capt. David Cowdin's company and Col. Benjamin Ruggles Woodbridge's regiment; he also served as corporal in the same company from May to August, 1775. "Massachusetts in the Revolution."

WILLIAM KIRBY was from Albermarle county, Virginia. He served in the Chesterfield militia. He removed to Harrison county, Kentucky, and from there to Somer, Champaign county, Illinois, where he died and is buried. He was pensioned.

NEWTON SHAW served in the war. No record of service has been obtained, but old residents of Champaign county remember hearing him say he served in the war.

Christian County

JONATHAN HICKLIN was born in Virginia in 1756. He removed to Kentucky, where his military service occurred in the war, as he acted as a spy in the Indian wars of that state. In 1813 he removed to Indiana, but later came to Wabash township, Clark county, Illinois, and from there to Christian county, where he died February 14, 1858, aged 102 years. He is buried in the Donner cemetery west of Owaneco. "County History and Records of Early Settlers."

Clay County

MOSES JOHNSON served in the Virginia troops, enlisting in 1777 under Capt. Alexander Morgan in Co. 2, Second Regiment, with Col. Alexander Spottiswood. He came to Clay county, Illinois, and died there, aged over 100 years. He was pensioned.

JOHN LEWIS served in the war from Virginia; he continued in the service after the close of the war. Coming to Illinois, he located in Clay county, and died there. The place of his burial is not known. "Pension Reports."

SAMUEL PARKS was from Virginia, where he served in the war. Coming to Illinois, he located in Clay county, where he died very aged, as he was 93 years of age in 1840. He was pensioned.

NATHANIEL WEST was born in Baltimore county, Maryland, May 6, 1750. He entered the service while living on Cross Creek, Virginia, in 1778, under Col. William Crawford, serving three months, during which time he assisted in building Ft. McIntosh. He also served in 1779 and 1780 with Capt. Matthew Richie and Col.

Crawford. He came to Lawrence county, Illinois, but removed to Clay county, where he died, aged over 90 years. He was pensioned.

Clark County

ZACHARIAH ARCHER was born in the county of Downs, Ireland, in 1752. He enlisted in 1776 from Northumberland county, Pennsylvania, in Capt. William Peebles' company, rifle regiment, commanded by Col. Samuel Miles. He was transferred to the Pennsylvania state regiment with Capt. Matthew Scott and Col. Walter Stewart. He was in the battles of Long Island, Trenton and Brandywine, also in camp at Valley Forge. He came to Illinois in 1819 and died in Clark county in 1822. He is buried in the Walnut Prairie cemetery. He was pensioned.

EBENEZER BARTLETT was born in Newberg, Orange county, New York, in 1757. He enlisted in 1775 and was in the battles of Harlem, White Plains and Ft. Montgomery, and was discharged in 1781. He came to Clark county, Illinois, in 1838 and died in December of that year. He is buried in the York cemetery and his grave has been marked by the D. A. R. of Marshall. He was pensioned.

NICHOLAS BEAN was born in Bucks county, Pennsylvania, March 16, 1760, and enlisted or was drafted, serving under Capt. John Lacy and Col. John Bull. After serving five months he enlisted in Col. Henry Lee's regiment, serving two years. He was in the battles of Guildford Court House, Cowpens, Eutaw Springs and the siege of Yorktown. He was wounded by a sabre cut across the head. He also served in the War of 1812. He lived in North Carolina, but came to Clark county, Illinois, in 1830, and died in 1838. He was pensioned.

THOMAS BOON was from North Carolina, where he was born in 1760. He served in the South Carolina troops. He came to Clark county, Illinois, and died there in 1836. He was pensioned.

HENRY BRISCOE was born in Maryland in 1763. He enlisted in 1781, serving until December under Capt. David Lynn and Major Alexander Roxburg. He was in the siege of Yorktown. He removed to Kentucky and from there to Clark county, Illinois, where he died, and is buried in the family burial ground one mile east of Westfield. He was pensioned.

PETER DOZIER was born in Virginia in 1762. He served in the Virginia troops. He came to Clark county, Illinois, where he died in 1838. He was pensioned.

ISAAC LATHROP was born in New York but served in the war from Massachusetts in Capt. Josiah Keith's company and Col. John Daggett's regiment for twenty-four days. He came to Clark county, Illinois, and there applied for a pension. "Massachusetts Soldiers in the Revolution."

THOMAS LAYTON was from Pennsylvania, where he served in the Northumberland county militia. He came to Clark county, Illinois, and died there after 1835. "Pennsylvania Archives."

SAMUEL McCLURE was born in Augusta county, Virginia, in 1748. He was a revolutionist before the Revolution, serving in 1774 and again in 1775 and 1781. He served under Capt. George Matthews, Capt. William Anderson, Capt. Thomas Smith and Capt. Zaccheus Johnson with Col. William Boyer and Col. Abraham Smith. His grave has been marked in Clark county. He was pensioned.

FREDERICK UNSELL was born in Pennsylvania, where he served in the war. He came to Clark county, Illinois, and died there in 1835, aged 70 years. He was pensioned.

Clinton County

JOHN CARRIGAN served in the war from Georgia. Coming to Illinois, he settled on Crooked Creek six miles east of Carlyle, Clinton county. He died and is buried on the land where he located. "Clinton County History."

ELIAS CHAFIN was a native of South Carolina, where he served in the war. He came to Illinois before 1825, settling in Clinton county in Sugar Creek precinct. He served on the grand jury in 1825. He was born in 1760. He was pensioned.

JOHN DUNCAN served in the war from Virginia. He removed to Kentucky and from there to Illinois, settling in the southwest part of Clinton county. He died in 1842 on the farm where he settled. He was pensioned.

JOHN KING served in the war from South Carolina. He came to Illinois in 1817, settling in Shoal Creek precinct, Clinton county. He was pensioned.

HUGH JOHNSON served in the war from North Carolina. After the war he removed to Kentucky, and in 1812 he came to Illinois, but removed to Missouri, returning to Clinton county, Illinois, settling near Trenton, where he died, aged 85 years. "North Carolina Records and Clinton County History."

MOSES LAND served in the war from Virginia. Coming to Illinois, he resided for a time in St. Clair county, but removed to Clinton county, where he died. He was pensioned.

THOMAS L. MOORE served with George Rogers Clark as a sergeant in Capt. Uriah Springer's company Virginia troops. He came to Clinton county, Illinois, where he applied for a pension. He received a grant of land for his service in the war. "Virginia Records."

WILLIAM MYERS served as a privateer in the Virginia troops. He removed to Clinton county, Illinois, where he applied for a pension. He was granted a tract of land for his war service. "Virginia Records."

PETER OUTHOUSE enlisted in Fredericktown, Maryland, in the Seventh Regiment, serving from August, 1780; again from October 26, 1780, under Lieut. Wm. Lamar and Capt. Lloyd Beall, in the ninth company, serving until November, 1783, when he was discharged. He removed to Kentucky, and in 1818 came to Clinton county, Illinois, settling in the southwest part of the county, where he died. He was pensioned.

JACOB SEAGRAVES enlisted in Granville county, North Carolina, in 1778, serving two and one-half years under Capt. Joseph Rhodes, Col. Dixon. He was in the battle of Eutaw Springs and several skirmishes. He removed to Tennessee, and from there to Clinton county, Illinois, where he died June 7, 1835. He was pensioned.

MICHAEL TEDRICH was from North Carolina. He was born at sea May 10, 1752. He enlisted in Anson county, North Carolina, serving three different times, three times each with Capts. William Hay, Solomon Wood and Robert High, under Col. Francis Malmedy. He came to Clinton county, Illinois, where he died February 10, 1834. He was pensioned.

Coles County

JONATHAN COLLOM was born in Montgomery county, Pennsylvania, December 10, 1760, and served as a musician in the war. In 1778 he was drafted for three months to fight the British under Capt. Marpole and Col. Dawling. In 1779 he was again drafted to serve in New Jersey with Capt. Dowling and Col. George Smith. He served both times as a musician and was paid as such. He again served as a Minute Man. When Cornwallis was marching through Virginia he again enlisted, but was taken sick and thus prevented from being present at the final surrender. After the close of the war he removed to Washington county, Tennessee, where he made application for a pension. He came to Illinois with his son William, settling in Coles county, where he died in the town of Charleston.

GEORGE COTTINGHAM was a native of Maryland, where he served in the war. He removed to Kentucky in early times, and in 1836 came to Coles county, Illinois, and died in Charleston. He was a shoemaker by trade and it is said he made boots for Washington. He died in 1860, aged 100 years. "County History."

ELISHA HADDEN was from North Carolina and served in the battle of King's Mountain and was wounded in a battle with the Cherokee Indians. For three months he lay in the fort helpless and was carried home to North Carolina on a litter. He came to Illinois and resided in Coles county, where he received a pension. He died there very aged. "County History."

JOSEPH FROST served in the Virginia line of troops. After the war he came to Illinois with his son and settled in Charleston, Coles county. When 87 years of age he received a pension for his service in the war. They came to Coles county in 1831.

JOHN HART was a native of Virginia. He served with George Rogers Clark in 1776 before coming to Illinois, and was in several battles with the Indians. He came to Illinois in 1826, coming from Hardin county, Kentucky, first to Wayne county, then to Coles county, Paradise township, where he died November 19, 1833. He was pensioned in 1831.

ISAAC KELLER was a soldier under Col. George Rogers Clark. He was a sergeant. He came to Coles county, Illinois, in 1820, where he died. (The names of soldiers who served with George Rogers Clark are to be found in the "William and Mary Quarterly" of Virginia.)

JOSEPH PAINTER was born in New Jersey in 1744. He served in the North Carolina troops, enlisting six times from 1777 to 1781, with Capts. William Bateman, John Turnbull, James Robinson, and .... Gillyfalls; under Cols. Bateman, Hugh Brevard, James Armstrong and Wm. Davidson. He was in the battle of Ramsour's Mill and several skirmishes with the Indians. He came to Illinois with his son and settled in the town of Hutton, Coles county. He was pensioned in 1833. He lived to be over 90 years of age.

JOHN PARKER was from Virginia, where he served in the war in Capt. Buller Claiborne's company, Col. Alexander Spottiswood's regiment, in 1777. He came to Coles county, Illinois, to reside, and died there. He was pensioned.

JAMES RYAN was a native of Virginia and enlisted there under Capt. James Calderwood, February 28, 1777, in the Eleventh and Fifteenth Virginia troops, Col. Daniel Morgan. He came to Illinois, settling in Coles county, where he was pensioned in 1831, aged 83 years. His place of burial is not known.

GRIFFIN TIPSOWARD was born in Pennsylvania in 1755. He enlisted in the county of Rowan, North Carolina, in 1775, serving in Gen. Griffith Rutherford's brigade, with Col. —— McKatty, Major Horn and Capt. Wm. Grimes. He was in the battle of Eutaw Springs under Gen. Nath. Greene; battle of King's Mountain under Col. Isaac Shelby; battle of Charleston under Col. McKatty and Capt. John McGuire. He resided in Kentucky and came from there to Coles county, Illinois, in 1810, settling in Hutton township, where he died. "County History."

Cook County

DAVID KENNISON was a "Revolutionist" before the Revolution, as he was the last survivor of the historic "Boston Tea Party." Upon the outbreak of the war he entered the service and served at the battles of Bunker Hill, West Point, White Plains, Long Island, Fort Montgomery, Staten Island, Delaware and Philadelphia, and was present at the surrender of Cornwallis. He was born in New Hampshire November 17, 1736, but removed to Maine with his father when very small. He also served in the second war for Independence. He voted for Washington, Madison, Monroe, Jackson, Van Buren and Polk. He was a strong "free soil" man and was active in the campaign. He died in Chicago February 24, 1852. On December 19, 1903, a granite boulder monument was unveiled in Lincoln Park, Chicago, which marks the place of his burial. This monument was erected by the Sons and Daughters of the American Revolution. The monument was unveiled by Dorothy Dayton Fessenden, daughter of Mrs. Benjamin Fessenden, regent of the Chicago chapter. "The Autobiography of David Kennison."

Crawford County

GEORGE BAITH was born in Lancaster county, Pennsylvania, in 1762. He enlisted in 1777 in the Pennsylvania troops, and was taken prisoner; was removed to a hospital on account of severe wounds. After he was recovered and released he again enlisted in Berkeley county, Virginia, in 1780, for three months, and again in 1781 for three months, serving as driver for baggage wagon in Gen. Anthony Wayne's army. He removed to Crawford county, Illinois, settling in Palestine. He died October 4, 1844, and is buried near Villas. He was pensioned.

PETER BARRACK served in the Maryland troops. He came to Crawford county, Illinois, and there applied for a pension. "Pension Reports."

SILAS BECKWITH was born in New Hampshire but served in the Massachusetts troops; was first lieutenant in Capt. Andrew

Lusk's company, in the Second Berkshire regiment. He was commissioned February 14, 1780. He removed to Crawford county, Illinois, and is probably buried in the county. He was pensioned.

WILLIAM DUNLAP was born in Laurens county, South Carolina, in 1760. He enlisted March, 1780, for six months with Capt. Joseph Pearson and Col. Casey. In 1781 he again enlisted for three months with Capts. Duval and Kenner Hudson; again he served in 1782 under Capt. Kenner Hudson. In 1818 he removed to Crawford county, Illinois, settling in Robinson township. He died July 2, 1835, and is buried near Villas. He was pensioned.

WILLIS FELLOWS served in the war from Massachusetts in Capt. Samuel Taylor's company and Col. Nicholas Dike's regiment in 1776. In 1777 he was with Capt. Lawrence Kemp's company and Col. Leeward's regiment, also with Capt. Benjamin Phillips and Col. Elisha Porter. He again enlisted in 1778, serving till December, 1779, and once enlisting in 1779, serving till 1780. He removed to Indiana, and from there to Crawford county, Illinois, where he died very aged. He was pensioned.

THOMAS GILL served as captain in the South Carolina troops. He was wounded at Savannah October 9, 1779, and again at Eutaw Springs September 8, 1781. He came to Illinois and for a time lived in Franklin county, but removed to Crawford county, settling four miles northwest of Palestine, where he died in 1840. He was pensioned.

DANIEL KENNEY served in the Virginia line of troops. He came to Crawford county,

Illinois, and died there August 9, 1824. He was pensioned.

ADAM KLEPINGER is said to have been a Revolutionary soldier, but no official record of service has been found. He is buried in Landes township, in the Klepinger cemetery. "Traditional Records."

THOMAS KINCAID was born in Ireland and came to America with the British army, but served in the Continental troops. He was at the battle of Bunker Hill, serving as orderly sergeant. He removed to Pennsylvania from New York, from there to Ohio, then to Kentucky, and from there to Indiana, and in 1840 came to Crawford county, Illinois, where he died at the advanced age of 105 years. "County History."

SAMUEL KINCAID came with his father and served as drummer boy at the battle of Bunker Hill. He was also in the War of 1812. He came with his father to Crawford county, locating in Montgomery township, and is probably buried there. He died aged 103 years. "County History."

OTHNIEL LOOKER was born in New Jersey, Morris county, in 1757. He enlisted in May, 1776, for one month; again for five months the same year, and again for one month under Capts. Obadiah Kitchell and David Bates, with Cols. Spencer and Ephraim Martin. He served again from 1777 to 1782, in all eighteen months, with Capts. Kitchell and Jonas Ward, under Col. Matthias Ogden. He was in the battles of Long Island and White Plains. He removed to Hamilton county, Ohio, and from there to Crawford county, Illinois. He died August 29,

1846, and is buried in the Kitchell cemetery. His grave is marked. He was pensioned.

DAVID McGAHY served in the war from Virginia. He came to Crawford county, Illinois, to reside. He was a prominent citizen, was a member of the state legislature. He died in September, 1851. "Virginia Records."

CONSTANTINE McMAHON was from Pennsylvania, where he served with Capt. John Brisben's company, Third Regiment. His period of service ended April 1, 1777. He came to Crawford county, Illinois, and died there; is buried in Landes township, in the Klipinger cemetery. "Pennsylvania Archives."

THOMAS PATTON was from North Carolina, but he was born at Marlboro, Pennsylvania, April 25, 1735. He enlisted in the North Carolina troops in 1779, serving six months with Capt. John Hardy and Col. Joseph McDowell. He served again in 1780 for six months with Col. William Campbell and again in 1781 for the same time with Capt. William Neal and Col. Campbell. He was in the battles of Ramsour's Mill, King's Mountain, Cowpens and Guildford Court House. He came to Crawford county and died there in Palestine township. He was pensioned.

ASA PIPER was from Massachusetts, where he served in the war, enlisting when only seventeen years of age. He served in Capt. Phineas Parker's company from Concord, serving six months from June 5, 1780, also from June, 1781. He came to Crawford county, Illinois, to reside, and probably died there. He was pensioned.

DAVID SHIPMAN served in the war from Virginia. He came to Crawford county, Illinois, and died there. "Virginia Records."

JOHN TAYLOR is said to have served in the war from Virginia, but as thirteen men from that state by the same name are recorded, it has not been determined which one came to Crawford county. "Traditional Records."

Dewitt County

EDWARD DAY was born in Charlotte county, Virginia, in 1760. He enlisted from that county in Capt. Charles M. Collier's company, Col. David Morgan's regiment, when only sixteen years of age, serving five months. He again served in Capt. William Price's company, Col. Thomas M. Randolph's regiment, serving three months, re-enlisting in Capt. Collier's company, Col. Randolph's regiment, he served three months; again enlisting he was in Capt. Gideon Spencer's company, Col. Randolph's regiment, serving two months, thus making a fine record of service for his country. He came to Illinois, settling in De Witt county, where he lies buried in De Witt cemetery. He died in 1836. Edward Day was the grandfather of Hon. W. H. Herndon, a law partner of Abraham Lincoln. "Virginia Records."

JOHN SCOTT was a native of Pennsylvania, born in York county, May 29, 1763. He enlisted from Washington county, Virginia, in May, 1780, in Capt. James Dysart's company, Col. William Gamble's regiment, Virginia line of troops, serving one year. He was in the battles of King's Mountain and Wetzell's Mills. The family came to Sangamon county, Illinois, in 1824; removed to De Witt county, where he died November 13, 1847, and is buried in Rock Creek cemetery, near Waynesville. "Virginia Records."

PETER CUTRIGHT, a native of Virginia, born in Hampshire county in 1759. He enlisted September 1, 1780, and served six months with Capts. Daniel Riteson and Robert Cravens, Col. Robert Stevens commanding. Peter Cutright came to Illinois and resided for a time in Macon county, his application for pension being from that county in 1833. He lived in Sangamon county until three years before his death, when he was a resident of De Witt county, where his last pension was drawn September 4, 1841. The place of his burial is not known.

WILLIAM VINCENT was born in Virginia and served from that state. Coming to Illinois, he settled at Long Point Timber, De Witt county. He applied for a pension in McLean county. He died in De Witt county in 1836, and is buried in Rock Creek cemetery. "Pension Reports" and "Virginia Records."

Du Page County

PARKER CHASE was a native of Connecticut. He served in the Revolutionary War, enlisting April 20, 1775, serving as a "Minute Man" in Capt. Thomas Noyes' company; also serving for thirteen weeks in Capt. Ezra Lunts' company, with Col. Moses Little's Seventeenth Regiment; again serving in Capt. Robt. Dodge's company, in Col. Ebenezer Travis' regiment; again enlisting with Capt. Jacob Powers and Capt. Stephen Jenkins, with Col. Jacob Gerrish, from Suffield and Essex counties, Connecticut. After the war Parker Chase came to Illinois, locating in Du Page county, where he died. He was pensioned.

JOHN DUDLEY was a native of New Hampshire, where he enlisted in Capt. Samuel Ashley's company in 1777, serving one month and two days, from September 21 to October 23. He came west from Claremont, New Hampshire, settling in Crawford county, and went ᐟfrom there to Du Page county, Illinois, where he died. He served as a justice in the county. He was pensioned.

THOMAS MATTESON was born in West Greenwich, Newport county, Rhode Island, in 1756. He enlisted June 8, 1776, with Lieut. George Tennant and Col. Nathan Brown. After the war he removed to Ashtabula county, Ohio, and from there came to Du Page county, Illinois. He lived to a great age and died in the county after 1840. He was pensioned.

Edgar County

ELIJAH AUSTIN was from Massachusetts, where he enlisted in Capt. John King's company, Col. Mark Hopkins' regiment. He enlisted July 15, 1776, serving sixteen days in Berkshire county. He came to Edgar county, Illinois, and died there; is buried near North Arm church. "Massachusetts Soldiers in the Revolution."

HUGH BARR was from Massachusetts, where he served three days in Col. James Converse's regiment; again for three days in Capt. Francis Starr's company. He again enlisted in September, same year (1777), serving sixteen days in Capt. Benjamin Nye's company, Col. Nathan Sparhawk's regiment, serving three months. He came to Edgar county and died there; is buried near Flemington. "Massachusetts Soldiers in the Revolution."

JAMES BENSON was from Talbot county, Maryland. He served as a sailor and after the war settled in Virginia. In 1824 he came with his son to Edgar county, Illinois. He is probably buried in the county, as his son removed to Jasper county in 1851. "County History."

GURDIN BURNHAM enlisted in Connecticut in 1775; he was on board the ship Alfred as a drummer, was captured in an engagement off Barbadoes and was exchanged in 1778. He came to Edgar county, but the place of burial is not known. He was pensioned.

ELIJAH CLAY enlisted from Virginia in 1780. He was in the battle of Guilford Court House. He removed to Edgar county, Illinois, but his place of burial is not known. He was pensioned.

JOHN CONREY enlisted from New York, where he served in the war; was in the battle of White Plains. Coming to Illinois, he settled in Edgar county at a place called Bloomfield Ledge. He died July, 1834, aged 84 years, and is buried in the Wynn graveyard. He was pensioned.

WILLIAM GANNON, SR., enlisted from North Carolina in 1780. He was in the battles of Camden, Guilford Court House, Eutaw Springs and Hughanne, where he was wounded. He died in Edgar county, Illinois, a very aged man. He was pensioned.

FERREL HESTER was from Maryland, where he enlisted in 1776; he again enlisted in the North Carolina troops in 1780, and was in the battles of Camden and Owans Ford. He came to Edgar county to reside and died there an aged man. He was pensioned.

WILLIAM HURST was born in Berkeley county, Virginia, in 1755. He enlisted in Westmoreland county, Pennsylvania, in July, 1780, in Capt. William Campbell's company, Col. Archibald Loughrey's regiment. They were to have joined George Roger Clark's expedition, but at Laughrey's Creek they were attacked by Indians, when both captain and colonel were killed. William Hurst was condemned to be burned, but was ransomed by McKee, a white chief, and was taken to Detroit, where he was a prisoner until May, 1781, when he was taken to a place near Montreal and was exchanged, arriving in New York about Christmas, 1781. After the war he removed to Kentucky, and from there to Indiana, and in 1836 he came to Edgar county, Illinois, where he died December 7, 1836. A monument was erected to his memory at Mount Carmel cemetery and inspiring dedicatory services were held. Among others who gave addresses was Prof. G. W. Brown, superintendent of schools, who has been most interested in gaining information regarding the soldiers buried in Edgar county. William Hurst was pensioned.

WILLIAM JAMES was from Maryland, where he enlisted July 20, 1776, by Michael Burgess. He enlisted again as corporal in the fourth regiment, eleventh company, serving from April, 1777, to November, 1780. He removed to Edgar county, Illinois, where he died and is buried near Asher church. "Maryland Records."

JAMES KNIGHT, SR., enlisted from Pennsylvania in 1775 and again a second time, serving on the frigate Randolph in 1776. His ship was in several engagements and captured three British ships. Coming to Illinois, he located in Edgar county and died on the farm where he located in Elbridge township. He was pensioned.

WILLIAM MEADOWS was from Maryland, where he served in the war, enlisting in 1776. He came to Edgar county, Illinois, to live, and died there. He is buried in the Prior cemetery. "Maryland Records."

WILLIAM MEANS enlisted in South Carolina in 1780. He was engaged in Gen. John Green's campaign of the south. He removed to Ohio, and from there to Edgar county, Illinois, locating in Paris township in 1822, where he is probably buried. He was pensioned.

ASA MOORE was from Maryland, where he enlisted in 1778. He was in the battle of Stony Point. After the war he removed to Pennsylvania and from there to Edgar county, Illinois. He was pensioned.

STEPHEN OGDEN served from Morris county, New Jersey, in the Eastern Battalion; was wounded September 13, 1777, at Second River. He was pensioned in Kentucky, Morgan county. He came to Edgar county, Illinois, and died there. He is buried on Tompkins farm, Edgar county. "New Jersey in the Revolution."

GEORGE REDMON was from Rowan county, North Carolina, where he enlisted, serving as a wagoner. He was in Gen. John Greene's campaign. Coming to Edgar county, Illinois, he settled in Paris township and is buried in a private graveyard about two miles south of Paris, in the Shelly Green farm. He was pensioned.

DANIEL RHODES was from Massachusetts, where he served in Capt. Samuel Payson's company, Col. John Graton's regiment, as a "Minute Man," enlisting April 19, 1775, for eight days; he again served for three months in Col. Joseph Read's regiment, and again in September, 1776, in a battalion stationed at Hull. He came to Edgar county, Illinois, and died there; is buried in the Ogden cemetery. "Massachusetts in the Revolution."

DANIEL ROWELL was from Connecticut, where he served in a regiment commanded by Capt. Jonathan Humphrey, Col. Samuel McClelland, in 1777. Coming to Illinois, he lived in Edgar county, in Elbridge township. He was pensioned.

WILSON THARP was from Virginia, where he served in the war. He came to Edgar county, Illinois, and there applied for a pension. "Virginia Records."

JOHN TUTWILER was from Virginia, where he served in the war. He came to Illinois and for a time resided in Coles county, but removed to Edgar county, where he died, and is buried in the Kansas cemetery. He was pensioned.

ABRAHAM WOOD was born February 7, 1753, in Frederick county, Maryland. He removed to North Carolina, where he enlisted, serving for six months from July, 1777, with Capts. John Johnson, James Chapman, and Col. Matthew Lock. He came to Edgar county to reside, where he applied for a pension. He died October 14, 1833, aged 80 years. He was pensioned.

Edwards County

JOHN FILES was born in England about 1758. Coming to America, he served in the war from South Carolina. He came to Illinois, settling in Wayne county in 1816, but removed to Edwards county, where he died. He was pensioned.

JOB PIXLEY was from Dighton county, Massachusetts, where he enlisted in 1775 with Capt. Peter Pitts and Col. Timothy Walker, serving over five years with these and other officers. He came to Wabash county, Illinois, settling first in Barney Prairie about 1809, later in Friendsville, but in 1829 he removed to Edwards county, where he died. He was pensioned.

BENJAMIN SMITH was born in England. He came from Alleghany county, New York, to Wabash county, Illinois, in 1816, settling in Lancaster precinct, but died in Edwards county in 1841. He served in the New York line of troops. He was pensioned.

Fayette County

JAMES CHESHIER was born in 1749 in Prince William county, Virginia. He served in the Virginia troops under Capts. William Farrow, Luke Cannon, John Hedges and Samuel Love and Col. Lee. He was in the battles of Brandywine, Gates' defeat, Williamsburg, Cowpens and Yorktown. He came to Illinois and located in Gallatin county, but died in Fayette county very aged. "Pension Reports."

JOSEPH EVANS was from Virginia, where he served in the war. He came to Fayette county in 1818, settling in Seminary township. He died September 4, 1832, and is buried in the Evans cemetery in Bear Grove township. He was pensioned.

JOHN MORRELL served in the war from Pennsylvania. He came to Fayette county, Illinois, and there applied for a pension. "Pennsylvania Archives" and "Pension Reports."

HENRY GINGER was born in Germany. He came to America when seven years of age. He enlisted when only sixteen years of age in the Pennsylvania troops and was taken prisoner at Charleston, South Carolina. He removed to North Carolina, then to Tennessee, and from there to Bowling Green, Fayette county, Illinois, in 1825. He died in 1842 and is buried in the Britton cemetery, six and one-half miles southeast from Vandalia. He was pensioned.

BENJAMIN TODD was from Maryland, enlisting there in the Fourth Regiment December, 1777, serving as sergeant. He came to Illinois and resided in Fayette county, where he died, and is buried in the Ables cemetery, just across the line from Montgomery county. "Maryland in the Revolution."

JAMES VERDEN was born in South Carolina August 25, 1756. He enlisted June 1, 1778, for three months under Capt. Francis Boykin, with Col. William Thompson. He removed to Missouri, but later came to Fayette county, Illinois, where he died June 18, 1843, aged 87 years. He was pensioned.

HENRY WALKER was from Virginia, where he served in the war. He came to Fayette county, Illinois, at an early day. He was a Baptist minister and preached in Wheatland township long before the first church was built at Loogotee, in 1851. He was a justice of the peace in Ramsey township. He died in 1832. He was pensioned.

Franklin County

ABEL DORTCH was from Mecklenburg county, Virginia; born about 1759. He served in the war from that state. After the war he removed to Tennessee, and from there to Franklin county, Illinois, where he died about 1835. He was pensioned.

SAMUEL GARDNER was from New York, where he served in the Fifth Regiment, New York troops, with Col. Lewis Du Bois; he again served under Col. Albert Pawling in the Dutchess county militia, in the Third Regiment. He came to Illinois and located in Franklin county, where he is probably buried. He was pensioned.

JOHN HOOKER served in the war from North Carolina, Granville county. Coming to Illinois, he lived in Franklin county, where he applied for a pension, but having served less than six months, it was not granted. "North Carolina in the Revolution."

MILLIAM McELYEA was from North Carolina and served in the Tenth Regiment, North Carolina troops, under Capt. Alexander Brevard, serving until March, 1783. He came to Franklin county, Illinois, and died there. He was pensioned.

JOSEPH MINZES was born April 9, 1755. He enlisted at Salisbury, North Carolina, in 1781, serving eighteen months with Capt. Edward Yarbrough's company in the Third Regiment, North Carolina troops. He came to Illinois and lived in Franklin county, where he died April 14, 1849. He was pensioned.

WILLIAM ROGERS served in the war from Virginia. He came to Franklin county, Illinois, where he applied for a pension, but having served less than six months it was not granted. "Virginia Records" and "Pension Reports."

SAMUEL TANNER was from North Carolina, where he served in the war. He came to Franklin county, Illinois, where he applied for a pension, which was not granted as he had served less than six months. "Pension Reports."

JOSHUA TYNER served in the war from Georgia. He came to Jackson county, Illinois, but removed to Franklin county, where he died. He was pensioned.

JACOB ZOLL was from Pennsylvania and served in the troops from that state. He came to Franklin county, Illinois, and there applied for a pension, but having served less than six months it was not granted. "Penna. Archives."

Fulton County

ROBERT BEER was born in Ireland April 21, 1750. He came to America in 1765, settling in Pennsylvania. He served in the war from Northampton county, sixth company, sixth battalion, commanded by Col. Jacob Stroud. He also was an Indian spy. He came to Fulton county, Illinois, and died there; is buried in the Beer graveyard in Young Hickory township, three miles west of Fairview. He was pensioned.

JONAS CLINE was born in Rochester, New York, June 25, 1760. He enlisted from Ulster county in 1780. He came at an early date to Fulton county, Illinois, and died there. He is buried in a private cemetery near Fairview. He was pensioned.

WILLIAM DOLLAR was born in Virginia in 1743. He enlisted October 15, 1776, serving until December 7, 1779, with Capts. Alexander Morgan, Marquis Chalmers and Thomas Collet, with Col. Christian Fehiger. He came to Fulton county, Illinois, and died there September 6, 1838. He was pensioned.

WILLIAM GRIFFITHS served in the New York troops in the Thirteenth Regiment, with Capt. Holter Dunham and Col. John McCrea. He came to reside in Fulton county, Illinois, and there applied for a pension. "New York in the Revolution."

JOHN HOWARD served in the Virginia troops. He came to Fulton county, Illinois, and there applied for a pension, but owing to a law passed by Congress in 1832 making the time of service necessary to be entitled to a pension six months, it was not granted. "Virginia Records."

JAMES KITCHEN served in the war from Northampton county, Pennsylvania, in the third company, under Capt. Hugh Gaston, Fifth Battalion, in 1781. Coming to Illinois, he settled in Fulton county, where he died, and is buried in the Old Temple cemetery near Table Grove. He was pensioned.

SAMUEL MALLORY was from Connecticut, where he served in the war in the Eighth Regiment under Capt. Comstock, from July, 1780, to December, 1780. He came to Fulton county, Illinois, and there applied for a pension, but not having served the required time, it was not granted. "Connecticut in the Revolution."

JOHN RITCHEY served in the war from Virginia with Capt. Benjamin Biggs. He came to Fulton county and there applied for a pension, but it was refused as he had served less than six months. "Virginia Records."

R. C. ROWLEY came to Fulton county, Illinois, and in 1840 he applied for a pension. He is doubtless the Reuben Rowley who served in the Fourth Regiment, New York line of troops from Albany, under Col. Kilian Van Rensselear He lived in Fulton county in what was then known as Pleasant township. "New York in the Revolution."

JACOB ULMER was from Orangeberg district, South Carolina, where he served in the war. Coming to Illinois, he settled in Fulton county, and asked for a pension, but had served less than six months and it was refused. "Pension Reports."

AUSTIN YANCEY served in the South Carolina troops from Greenville county. He came to Fulton county, Illinois, and applied for a pension, but having served less than six months, it was not granted. "Pension Reports."

CHRISTOPHER ZOLL was a native of Maryland, where he doubtless served in the war. He came to Fulton county, Illinois, and applied for a pension at the age of 88 years. He probably died before the pension was granted. He is buried near Fairview. "Pension Records of 1840, which were gathered by the marshalls of the district and cannot always be verified."

JOHN BIVENS was born September 15, 1760, in Middletown, Connecticut. He enlisted in March, 1775, for nine months as a fifer in Capt. Jacob Allen's company, Col. Jonathan Brewer's Massachusetts regiment. He again enlisted in December, 1775, for one year, with Capt. Aaron Haynes and Col. Asa Whitcomb. In August, 1777, he served for two years under Capt. Ebenezer Webber, and in 1779 he again served for three months with Capt. Gideon King in the New York line of troops. He removed to Ohio, and from there to Fulton county, Illinois, where he died February 24, 1839, and is buried at Marrietta. His widow drew his pension after his death. He was pensioned.

GEORGE HAINLINE, SR., served in the war from one of the Carolinas. He removed to Illinois, settling in Fulton county, where he is buried. Descendants give his service in the battle of King's Mountain. "Traditional Records."

Gallatin County

WILLIAM ABNEY served in the war from Virginia. He also continued in the service of the United States after the close of the war. He came to Gallatin county, Illinois, and is doubtless buried in that county. "Virginia Records."

WILLIAM ALLEN was born in Pennsylvania but enlisted in North Carolina, serving in both cavalry and infantry. He was sergeant in 1781 under Lieut. John Campbell and Ensign Robert Scoby, with Col. Archibald Lytle. He was taken prisoner at Hillsburg but exchanged August 11, 1782, and returned to his home in Orange county. He came to Gallatin county and is doubtless buried there. He was pensioned.

STEPHEN BOUTWELL served in the Virginia troops under Capt. Samuel Hawes and Col. Alexander Spottiswood from January 1, 1777, to June the same year, acting as corporal.

He came to Gallatin county, Illinois, and is probably buried there. He applied for a pension. "Virginia Records."

GREENBERRY CHOATE was born in Virginia in 1751. He served one month in 1779 under Capt. William Cocke and Col. Andrew Christie, in the North Carolina troops. He again enlisted in July, 1780, for four months under Capt. James Lawrence and Col. Andrew Christie. He again served one month with Capt. Ezekiel Smith and Col. Thomas Clark in 1781. He came to Johnson county, Illinois, but died in Gallatin county in 1842, and is buried on Eagle Creek, near Equality. He was pensioned.

JOHN DUFF was a Virginian. He gave George Rogers Clark valuable information regarding Kaskaskia when the soldiers were on their way to that place. In 1805 he was on his way to Virginia and was killed on Ripple Island, Gallatin county, and was buried near the old salt springs. "County History."

ABNER FOSTER was from Massachusetts, where he served in Capt. Benjamin Adams' company, Col. Jonathan Johnson's regiment, enlisting August 15, 1777, serving four months. He came to Gallatin county, Illinois, and is doubtless buried there as he was an aged man. He was pensioned.

BENNET HANCOCK served in the Virginia troops, for which he was granted 100 acres of bounty land. He was born in 1756 and served under Col. Christian Fehiger. He came to Gallatin county, Illinois, and died there April 7, 1833. He was pensioned, and his widow drew the pension after his death. "Virginia Records" and "Pension Reports."

WILSON HENDERSON was from Chester county, South Carolina, and served in the war from that state. He came to Gallatin county, Illinois, and is probably buried in the county. "Pension Reports."

JOHN LAMB, SR., was from North Carolina, where he served in the war in the Tenth Regiment, North Carolina troops, under Capt. James Mills, from January, 1782, to January, 1783. He removed to Gallatin county, Illinois, and settled near Ridgeway, where he is probably buried as he was an aged man when he applied for a pension. He was pensioned.

JAMES NORTON was in the war from Virginia. He continued in the service in the Sixth U. S. Infantry. He came to Gallatin county, and is probably buried there. "Virginia Records."

GEN. THOMAS POSEY was born in Virginia July 9, 1750. He is said to have been the natural son of George Washington, his mother being Elizabeth Lloyd. He served as captain in the Seventh Virginia Regiment; in 1776 was promoted to a major in Col. Daniel Morgan's regiment. He was made lieutenant-colonel, and after the close of the war was made brigadier-general. He was in the battles of Monmouth, Stony Point, and was at Yorktown. In 1794 he removed to Kentucky, where he was a Senator in 1805-06. He also served in the War of 1812. He was governor of Indiana Territory, serving until it was made a state in 1816. He removed to Illinois, settling in Gallatin county, where he died March 18, 1818. He is buried near Shawneetown, and his grave is marked by a monument, though it is in a decaying condition.

"Virginia Records" and "The National Cyclopedia of Biography."

WILLIAM SUTTON was born in Virginia in 1764. He served in 1781 for two months under Capt. John Jackson and Col. Thomas Merriwether; he again served for six months with Capt. Thomas Eaton, and Col. William Darke. He was at the battle of Yorktown. He came to Gallatin county, Illinois, and died there. He was pensioned.

JOHN THADOWEN was a resident of Gallatin county, Illinois, and in 1840 was 85 years of age when he applied for a pension. It is not known from what state he served as the records of that time are not complete. "The 1840 Pension Reports."

ROBERT WEST was from Bertie county, North Carolina, where he served in the war. He came to Gallatin county, Illinois, and there applied for a pension. "North Carolina in the Revolution" and "Pension Records."

In 1825 Gen. Lafayette visited Gallatin county. On this occasion a poorly clad Frenchman stood at the door of the hotel looking at Lafayette. As soon as Lafayette saw him he advanced to greet him with both hands extended. He was an old soldier who had served as a bodyguard for Lafayette. "County History."

Greene County

MICHAEL M. BAKER was born in 1753 in Borough of Southwark, London, England. He came to America in 1773 and espoused the cause of the new country. He enlisted in 1779 in Major Frederick Vernon's company, Col. David Broadherdin, Pennsylvania troops, serving as sergeant. He removed to Ohio and later to Greene county, Illinois, where he died in 1831. He was pensioned.

WILLIAM BEMAN was born May 2, 1758, at Kent, Connecticut. He enlisted June 1, 1776, for six months with Col. Heman Swift and Capt. Ebenezer Couch. In 1777 he again served for two months with Capt. Sackett and Col. Hooker, and served again in the same year for two months with Capt. Peter Mills and Col. John Wood. He served the fourth time in 1779 for six months with Col. Heman Swift. He came to Greene county, Illinois, and died there October 21, 1837. He was pensioned.

ALLEN J. BRIDGES was a native of Wake county, North Carolina, born in 1756. He enlisted in Rowan county and served seven month as private in Capt. Simeon Alexander's company, Col. Joseph McDowell's regiment. He was in the battles of Ramsour and Salisbury. He married in Greene county, Elizabeth Irwin, and after his death she drew his pension. He was buried in the Woodbury cemetery, Kane township. He was pensioned.

JOHN CLARK was born in 1765 in Lancaster county, Pennsylvania. He served from 1778 to the close of the war, enlisting three different times, with Capts. Timothy Downing, Samuel Teeters and Cols. Matthew Williamson and William Crawford, in the Virginia line of troops. He was in battle with Indians at the time Col. Crawford was captured. He came to Greene county, Illinois, and died there September 13, 1844. He was pensioned.

JESSE CONWAY was from Virginia, where he enlisted at Reed Island in 1777 for eighteen months, and again in 1779 for sixteen months under Capts. William Buchanan and Isaac Riddle with Cols. Boon and Abraham Bowman. He died in Greene county, aged 79 years. He was pensioned.

JOHN FLATT served in the war from Middlesex county, New Jersey. He came to Greene county and there applied for a pension, but not having served six months it was not granted. "New Jersey in the Revolution."

JAMES GARRISON was born near Fredericktown, Pennsylvania, in 1747. He enlisted in Wilkes county, North Carolina, in 1775 for three months under Capt. John Hamlin, Col. Benjamin Cleveland; enlisted again in 1781 with Capt. Alexander Gordan, Col. Joseph McDowell. He was in the battles of Cross Creek, the surrender of Ninety-six, and Eutaw Springs. He came to Greene county, Illinois, and died there very aged; is buried in the Patterson cemetery. He was pensioned.

ADONIJAH GRISWOLD was born at New Milford, Connecticut, in 1758. He entered the service in Vermont under Capt. Joshua Barnum and Major Gideon Brownson, Vermont militia, serving as a scout until 1778, when he was taken prisoner and carried to Quebec; was kept there until 1781. He came to Greene county, Illinois, and died there September 1, 1841; is probably buried in White Hall. "Vermont in the Revolution."

JOHN HEWITT was born in Brunswick county, Virginia. He removed to North Carolina, where he enlisted in August, 1778; he re-enlisted seven times, serving until 1781; he was a sergeant under seven captains, viz., James Williams, Ballard Smith, William McFarlane, James Moore, John Henderson, Nathan Goodye,

Richard White, John Fuller and Col. Francis Malmady. He was in the battles of Guildford Court House and Ramsour's Mill. He came to Greene county, Illinois, and died there in 1848; is buried in the Providence cemetery, East Carrolton. He was pensioned.

ROBERT LORTON was born in Charlotte, Virginia, where he enlisted in 1776, serving two years in the Fourth Virginia Regiment under Capt. John Morton and Col. Adam Stephen. He was in the battles of Trenton, Germantown and Brandywine. He enlisted again under Capt. John Holcomb, serving six months. After the war he removed to Kentucky, and at an early date came to Illinois, locating in Bond county, but later in Greene county, where he died in 1833. Robert Lorton was the founder of Lorton Prairie, near Whitehall, where he lies buried. He was pensioned.

FRANCIS MILLER was born at sea October 16, 1753, when his parents were on a voyage from Philadelphia to Charleston, South Carolina. They were in Mecklenburg county, where he enlisted in 1775 as private. He was made captain, serving three times as that officer in the Riflemen Rangers with Col. Robert Irwin. He served until 1781 and was in the battles of Hanging Rock and Guildford Court House. He came to Greene county, Illinois, at an early date and died there in 1843. He is buried in the North cemetery, Greenfield. He was pensioned.

JOHN A. MILLER was from Orange county, Virginia, where he enlisted, serving from April, 1778, to September, 1778, in company No. 5 with Col. Thomas Marshall in the Third Regiment. He came to Greene county, Illinois, where he applied for a pension, but not having served six months, it was not granted. "Virginia Records."

CALEB POST was a native of New Jersey, where he served in the war from Morris. He also served in the state troops. Coming to Illinois, he settled in Greene county, and is probably buried in Bluffdale. He was pensioned.

THOMAS RICHARDSON served in the war from Virginia. He continued in the service after the close of the war and was in the United State infantry. He came to Greene county, Illinois, and probably died there. "Virginia Records."

JONAH SCROGGINS was born in Brunswick county, Virginia, but enlisted in Burke county, North Carolina, in 1778, with Capt. Robert Temples and Major Charles Pickney. He re-enlisted three times under Capts .Philip Taylor, Philip Thomas and John Whitley, with William Dennis and Robert Rayford as majors. He came to Greene county, Illinois, where he died in 1845; is probably buried in Carrolton. He was pensioned.

AARON SMITH was born in 1765 in North Carolina. He enlisted there in 1781, only serving thirty-four days, when he was shot through the thigh in the battle of Eutaw Springs. He served under Capts. Elijah Moore and Michael Randolph, with Cols. Archibald Lytle and Henry Lee. He removed to Tennessee, and from there to Greene county, Illinois, where he died in March, 1841, and is probably buried in Roodhouse. He was pensioned.

WILLIAM THAXTON was from Caswell county, North Carolina, where he served in the war from May, 1782. He came to Greene county, Illinois, where he applied for a pension. "North Carolina Records."

JOHN THOMPSON was born in Botetourt county, Virginia. He enlisted in 1781 for three months with Capt. Henry Pawling, Col. William McClenahan. He again served for five months and again for one month in 1781 under Capt. David May, Col. Thomas Fleming, in the Virginia troops. He came to Greene county, Illinois, where he died March 27, 1843, and is buried in the Thompson graveyard, Burrow township. He was pensioned.

GEORGE VINCINER served in the war in the Kentucky artillery. He came to Greene county, Illinois, where he probably died. He was pensioned.

Hamilton County

JACOB BARKER served in the Pennsylvania troops in Capt. John Rea's company. He was of Irish parentage. The family history gives an account of his service, that after serving one year he was wounded in the hip and was discharged, but upon his recovery he re-enlisted and was again wounded in the leg. He came to Hamilton county, Illinois, and died on the farm where he had lived for many years, between the towns of Walpole and Broughton. "Pennsylvania Archives" and "Family History."

GRANDFATHER DAVIS, a soldier of the American Revolution, lies buried in Hamilton county. Old residents have vouched for this information. His given name is not known, or the state from which he served. "Traditional Records."

FRANCIS DOLAHIDE was born in Caswell county, North Carolina, in 1750. He served for six years, enlisting early in 1776 for three months, again for three months, again after two weeks for three months, and again in 1781 serving to the close of the war. He served under Capts. William Morrow, Small, Christopher Taylor and Samuel Sexton, with Col. Archibald Lytle and Major Dugan. He was in the battles of Eutaw Springs and Yorktown. Coming to Illinois, he located in Hamilton county, where he died August 30, 1837. He was pensioned.

GEORGE FITZGERALD served from Virginia. He was discharged from the service May 24, 1780. He was in Col. John Gibson's detachment in the western department. He came to Hamilton county, Illinois, and died there; is buried in the Gatlin cemetery, Crouch township, on the farm of Felix C. Upchurch. "Pennsylvania Archives" and "Family History."

AMBROSE MAULDING was born in Virginia August 1, 1735. He served in the Virginia troops. He came to Hamilton county, Illinois, and died there August 25, 1833, and is buried near McLeansboro, near the "Ten-Mile Baptist Church." A granddaughter is still living who attended his funeral. His grave is marked by a substantial monument which bears the following inscription: "Immortal may their memory be who fought and died for Liberty." "Virginia Records" and "Family History."

FREDERICK MAYBERRY served in the war from Virginia. He came to reside in Hamilton county, Illinois, and there applied for a pension, but not having served six months, it was not granted. He is buried in Big Hill cemetery. "Virginia Records" and "County History."

51

RANDLE McDANIEL was born in Frederick county, Maryland, in 1755. He removed to South Carolina, where he served three months in 1775 under Capt. John Patton and Col. Holt Richardson. He removed to White county, Illinois, but died in Hamilton county. He was pensioned.

LITTLE PAGE PROCTOR was born in Granville county, Virginia, in 1760. He enlisted with Capt. Cornelius Riddle, serving from March, 1778, to the close of the war, and was retained in service until August, 1794. He came to Hamilton county, Illinois, and died there November 15, 1852, aged 92 years. He is buried in the Concord cemetery, near McLeansboro. He was pensioned.

NICHOLAS PROCTOR was doubtless a brother of Little Page Proctor, and served in the Virginia troops. He was born in 1755 and died in Hamilton county. He was pensioned.

JESSE TAYLOR was born in England, but coming to America he enlisted with the Colonists, serving with the Virginia troops. Coming to Illinois, he settled near Olga, Hamilton county. He is buried near the town of Walpole. His widow drew a pension for many years. "Family History" and "Virginia Records."

HENRY J. WILLIAMS served from Virginia during the war, and was continued in the service in the United States infantry after the close of the war. He removed to West Tennessee and from there to Hamilton county, Illinois. His burial place is not known. "Virginia Records."

Hancock County

To Hancock county belongs the credit of erecting the first tablet in the state in memory of Revolutionary soldiers buried in that county. On July 2, 1910, the Shadrach Bond Chapter, Daughters of the American Revolution of Carthage, unveiled a tablet bearing the names of seven soldiers. The regent, Mrs. John Lawton, was chairman of the day. After the invocation, the "Star Spangled Banner" was sung, followed by an address by Hon. Charles S. DeHart; then "Illinois" was sung. The tablet was presented to the county by Mrs. Lawton and was accepted by Mr. John MacKelvie, president of the Board of Supervisors. A lineal descendant of David Baldwin, Miss Phoebe Ferris, unveiled the tablet. The singing of "Hail Columbia" closed the exercises.

DAVID BALDWIN was born in Dutchess county, New York, May 5, 1761. He enlisted when a mere lad, being but fifteen years of age, serving as private in the Third Regiment, under Col. John Field in the New York line of troops. He was in the service ten months, from February to December. He died April 29, 1847, and is buried in Carthage. He was pensioned.

CHARLES BETTISWORTH was born in Virginia in 1761. He enlisted when only eighteen years of age, three years after the battle of Lexington, and served until the close of the war in the Virginia line of troops. He came to Illinois at an early date, settling in Hancock county, where he died June 12, 1842; is buried in the Bethel cemetery. He was pensioned.

SAMUEL CALDWELL was a native of Virginia, born near Wheeling in 1749. He served in the Virginia line of troops, being chief of scouts. He came to Illinois after the close of the war, settling in Hancock county, where he died in 1850 at the advanced age of 101 years. He is buried on the Brenneman farm between Chili and Stillwell, Hancock county. He was pensioned.

JOHN LIPSIE was born in 1732 and died in Hancock county in 1835, being 103 years of age. He is buried in the Belknap cemetery. He served from Virginia. He was pensioned.

UTE PERKINS served in the war from South Carolina. Coming to Illinois he lived in Hancock county, and there applied for a pension. He had not served six months and it was not granted. "Pension Records."

RICHARD ROSE was born in 1754. He died in Hancock county, February 14, 1842, aged 88 years, and is buried in Lot 9, Range B, in Pulaski cemetery, near Augusta. He served in the Virginia line of troops, and was pensioned.

ALEXANDER K. PATTERSON was born in New York; date unknown. He served in the Orange county militia, in the Fourth Regiment, under Col. John Hathorn. He died in Hancock county, and is buried on the Cozard farm, south of Elvaston. Patterson, New Jersey, was named for a son of Alexander Patterson. "New York in the Revolution."

ASA WORTH was born in Leicester, Mass., August 25, 1763, and died in Hancock county, Illinois, February 15, 1845. He is buried in Nauvoo. He applied for a pension which was held for further specification. Descendants vouch for his service.

Henderson County

BENJAMIN BLANKENSHIP was from Hampton, Virginia. He enlisted in 1777, serving in Capt. Anthony Singleton's company, and Col. Charles Harrison's regiment. He was in the battle of Camden. He removed to Ohio and in 1836 came to Warren county, Illinois. He died in 1844 and is buried in Henderson county. He was pensioned.

SAMUEL CHAPIN was from Vermont, where he served in 1777 in Capt. Parmelee Allen's company; he also served from June 16 to July 10, 1778, in Capt. Samuel Robinson's company, and Col. Samuel Herrick's regiment. He again served in Capt. Joseph Safford's company, and Col. Ebenezer Walbridge's regiment, from August 2, to August 8, 1781. He removed to New York, then to Pennsylvania, and from there to Indiana, and about 1839 to Knox county, Illinois. He died in Henderson county, and is buried in the Oquaka cemetery. He was pensioned.

DAVID FINLEY was born in Belfast, Ireland, March 9, 1761. Coming to America when a lad, he enlisted in Capt. Samuel Miller's company, and Col. Aeneas Mackey's Eighth Regiment, Pennsylvania troops. He was in the battles of Brandywine and Germantown. In 1818 he was in Clarke county, Indiana, but removed to Warren county, Illinois. He died September 3, 1838, and is buried near Oquaka, Henderson county. He was pensioned.

EARL FRIZZELL was from Massachusetts, where he served in the war. He came to Henderson county, Illinois, where he applied for a pension. "Pension Reports."

DAVID LYNN was born in Connecticut in 1764; he enlisted in 1780 under Capt. Marvin Lord, and Lt. William Lynn (his brother), in

Col. Herman Swift's regiment. About 1832 he removed to Warren county, Illinois. He is buried near the Old South Henderson Presbyterian Church. He was pensioned.

DANIEL McMILLAN was a soldier from South Carolina. He was born in 1752, and died in Henderson county, Illinois, August 1, 1838. "Family Records."

Henry County

GEORGE NIXON enlisted December 15, 1776, for three months, as Ensign with Capt. George Evans, and Col. Thomas Duff in the Delaware troops. He re-enlisted for six weeks in the same company, and was chosen Lieutenant October 15, 1777, serving from October 15, 1777, until July, 1778, under Capt. David McKee, and Col. Thomas Duff. He was in the battles of Princeton and Brandywine. He removed to Ohio, and from there to Rock Island county, Illinois, August 15, '841. His grandson is still living and remembers his grandfather well. He is buried about twenty miles east of Rock Island, in the Green River district. He was pensioned.

Iroquois County

THOMAS WILLIAMSON was born in Hampshire county, Virginia, in 1757. He served one year before the close of the war under Capt. John Anderson, Col. —— commanding. He also made gun powder for the use of the army. He removed to Ohio, and in 1825 to Indiana, and in 1832 he came to Illinois, settling in Crab Apple township, Iroquois county, where he died. He was pensioned.

Jackson County

DANIEL BANOW, or Barrow, was born in 1757 in Brunswick county, Virginia. He enlisted in Virginia in 1776 for three months under Capt. John Williamson in Virginia troops. He enlisted again in the North Carolina troops, with Capts. John Hill, Francis Tartanson, and Col. James Hogan, serving thirteen months. He was in the battle of Guilford Court House. He came to Jackson county, Illinois, and died there. He was pensioned.

ROBERT FRY was from Virginia where he served with Capt. Bembridge Goodwin. He removed to Jackson county, Illinois, and died there He was pensioned.

ROBERT FRIATT served in the Virginia line of troops. He came to Jackson county, Illinois, and settled in Ridge township, at Dutch Ridge, before 1812. He is probably buried in Jackson county. He was pensioned.

JESSE GORDON was born in Virginia, October 3, 1755. He enlisted in 1776 in the North Carolina troops, as Orderly-Sergeant, under Capt. William Shepherd and Col. Joseph Williams, serving three months. He removed to Wilkes county, Georgia, and served there in 1777, as First Lieutenant with Capt. James Hawkins, and Col. John Stewart, serving eleven months. He served again in 1778 under Capt. John Gunnells and Col. John Dooley. He again enlisted under Col. Elijah Clarke, and was in the battle at Kettle Creek. In the winter of 1780 and 1781 he was taken prisoner, but paroled. He broke his parole and aided in driving the British out of Augusta, but was captured, and a prisoner until 1782, when he again escaped, returning to Wilkes county and there was again captured and kept for eight months, when he was freed. Returning home he continued in the service until 1783, when peace was declared. He served fighting the Indians after the close of the war. A wonderful record of a brave soldier. He came to Jackson county, Illinois, and died there August 27, 1850. He was pensioned.

ZACHARIAH LYRELY was born June 2, 1755, in Culpepper county, Virginia. He enlisted in Rowan county, North Carolina, in 1777, for three months with Capt. George H. Berger; in 1778 for five months under Capt. Thomas Cook, and again for six months with Capt. Richard Grimes, and Col. Robert Rutherford. He came to Jackson county at an early day, settling at Dutch Ridge. He was in the battles of Reedy Fork and Guildford Court House. He was pensioned.

EBENEZER PYATT was born in Pennsylvania in 1755. He enlisted in Virginia, serving four years. He removed to Ohio, and from there to Tennessee, then to Kentucky, and in 1814 to Jackson county, Illinois, settling at Dutch Ridge. He doubtless died there. He was pensioned.

JOSEPH J. WILLIAMS was from Pennsylvania, where he served in the war. He came to Jackson county, Illinois, settling in Elk township in the northern precinct, in 1815. He was pensioned.

Jersey County

WILLIAM BATES was born in Pennsylvania in 1759. He served in the First South Carolina Regiment, commanded by Col. Charles Pinckney, from April 14, 1776, to December, 1776.

Coming to Illinois in 1835, he located in Madison county, where he died February, 1848, but was buried at Jersey Landing, now Elsah, Jersey county. He was pensioned.

JONATHAN COOPER was born in Maryland, but served in the war in Pennsylvania as a drummer. He removed to Kentucky and came to Illinois in 1835, settling four miles southwest of Jerseyville, where he died August, 1845. He was pensioned while living in Kentucky.

WILLIAM GILLHAM was one of the famous Gillham family of sons, who served in the war from South Carolina. He came to Madison county, Illinois, with his brothers, but removed to Jersey county, where he died. "Family History" and "County Records."

Jefferson County

DANIEL CHANDLER was from South Carolina, where he served in the Ninety-sixth District, February, 1776, under Capt. Jarret Smith, for four months. He again served in May, 1777, with Capt. James Lisle and Col. Jonas Beard, for two months, and one month with Capt. Frederick Lipham. In 1778 and 1779 he served with Capt. James Lisle and Col. John Lisle for over four months. He again served in June, 1780, with Capt. William Smith and Col. John Thomas; was in the battles of Cedar Springs, and Musgrove Mill, and in constant service until the close of the war. He was made Lieutenant under Capt. Jeremiah Williams and Col. John Hammond. He came to Jefferson county, Illinois, where he died. He was pensioned.

FRANCIS HANEY was born in Prince Edward county, Virginia, April 19, 1754. He enlisted in Botetourt county, serving from June, 1776, to December, 1776, under Capt. Daniel Smith. He again served from September, 1778, for seven months with Capt. George Adams, again for three months with Col. Isaac Shelby, and once more for nine months with Capts. George Maxfield, Robert Caldwell, and John Martin. He came to Morgan county, Illinois, but died in Jefferson county. He was pensioned.

SAMUEL LITTLE was from South Carolina where he served in the war, being in the Cavalry. He was born in 1765. He came to Jefferson county, Illinois, and died there. He was pensioned.

WILLIAM LONG was born August 9, 1756, near Mt. Vernon, the home of Washington. He served in the Virginia troops and was in the battles of Brandywine and Germantown. He came to Illinois and lived in Mt. Vernon, Jefferson county. It is said that he was one of Washington's body guards. "Virginia Records" and "County History."

JOHN MURPHY served in the war from North Carolina. He came to Illinois in 1818. He died very aged, probably in Jefferson county. "North Carolina Records and County History."

JOEL PACE was born in Virginia, July 28, 1762. He served in the war from that state. He removed to Kentucky and later to Jefferson county, Illinois, settling in Mt. Vernon township where he died. "Virginia Records" and "County History."

THOMAS WILLIAMS was from North Carolina, where he served in the war, serving in both Infantry and Cavalry. He came to Illinois when it was a Territory, settling in Jefferson county, where he probably died. He was pensioned.

Jo Daviess County

REV. SAMUEL MITCHELL was born in Cecil county, Maryland, in 1760. He removed to Botetourt county, Virginia, where he served in the war. He came to Illinois in 1817, settling near Belleville, St. Clair county. It is probable that he was the "Rev. —— Mitchell" who opened the Constitutional Convention in 1818, with prayer. He and his brother Edward built a church in Bellville. He removed to Galena and lived to a great age, preaching when he was 80 years of age. He died near Galena. "Virginia Records" and "St. Clair County History."

Johnson County

DANIEL CHAPMAN was born in Westchester county, New York, July 25, 1756. He enlisted in 1775 for nine months under Capt. Richard Sackett and Col. John Thomas. One year later, in the Spring of 1776, he again enlisted for nine months and rendered most efficient service against the Tories, who were numerous in that county. In 1777 he acted as scout and was appointed second Sergeant under Col. Frederick Weisenfeldt, serving one year. In August, 1781, they marched south to meet Lord Cornwallis in Virginia. He removed to Johnson county, Illinois, and died there February 8, 1841, and is buried east of Vienna, on his farm. A monument erected by his family marks his grave. A most faithful soldier of the American Revolution. He was pensioned.

JACOB HARWICK was born in Pennsylvania in 1752. He served three months in 1781 under Capt. Thomas Hewitt, in Col. Joseph Phillips' regiment in the North Carolina troops.

He again enlisted under Capt. Charles Gordon, and served one year. He removed to Johnson county, Illinois, and died there in 1833. He is buried two miles east of Vienna. A government marker has been placed at his grave by the Vienna D. A. R. He was pensioned.

RANDOLPH LAWSON was born in Cumberland county, North Carolina, in 1752, where he enlisted in 1780 under Capt. Cox or Gholston, guarding baggage during the battle of Camden. He again enlisted in 1781 and during the battle of Guildford Court House guarded baggage. He removed to Kentucky and from there to Johnson county, Illinois, where he applied for a pension, but having served less than six months, it was not granted. "Pension Reports."

HEZEKIAH WEST was born in Maryland, November 7, 1763. He enlisted in the South Carolina troops in Capt. Robert Frost's company, in Col. Richard Winn's regiment, for one month, and again for three months in same company. He again enlisted in 1782 with Capt. John McCoot's company of mounted rangers, in Col. David Hopkins' regiment for three months. His father served in the same company and was killed in 1778. Hezekiah West was a member of the Illinois State Convention in 1818 from Johnson county. He died July 29, 1845, and is buried in the West Eden cemetery, Johnson county. His grave is marked by a government marker. He was pensioned.

WILLIAM WIGGS was born in North Carolina in 1758. He enlisted in Wayne county, serving for thirty-five days in 1775, in Capt. William Fellows' company. He again enlisted in 1779 for five months with Capt. John Canada, and in

1781 he served three months under Capt. Joseph Sessions and was in the battle of Guilford Court House. He removed to Johnson county, Illinois, and died there in 1835. He was pensioned.

Kane County

WILLIAM BENNETT was born at Sandown, New Hampshire, May 9, 1758. He enlisted four different times; first, August, 1776, under Capt. Nathan Brown and Col. Pierce Long, New Hampshire troops; second, 1779, with the same officers; the third time in 1780 under Col. Timothy Bedel, in Massachusetts troops, with Capt. Charles Johnson and Col. James Wadsworth; fourth time, September, 1782, with Capt. Cutting Farror, New Hampshire troops. He was in the battle of Fort Ann. He removed to New York, Genesee county, and from there to Kane county, Illinois, in 1836, where he died February 15, 1846, and is buried near Wasco, in a private cemetery. He was pensioned.

NATHAN BROWN was from New York, where he enlisted in Weschester county, under Capt. Benjamin Chapin, and Col. Thaddeus Crane. He came to Kane county, Illinois, where he died and is buried in Batavia township. He was pensioned.

DANIEL BURROUGHS was from New York where he enlisted in the Charlotte county Militia with Capt. Elshama Tozer, and Cols. Alexander Webster, and Thomas Armstrong in the Dorset Regiment. He was pensioned.

ABNER POWERS was born in Richmond, New Hampshire, December 15, 1760. He enlisted January 1, 1777, serving until December, 1781, under Col. John Stark, and again in the Seventh Company, 1778, for two years with Capt.

William Farwell. He came to Kane county, Illinois, where he died October 19, 1852, and was buried at Lily Lake, Virgil township. A marble slab bore the inscription "A Soldier of the Revolution," also a sword carved in the marble. Several years since it was ascertained that the stone was broken, and it was determined to erect a suitable monument to the memory of Abner Powers, who had been in the battles of Bennington, Saratoga, Valley Forge, and Yorktown. The monument stands thirty feet high, and was dedicated with impressive ceremonies, three companies of the Third State Regiment and five hundred members of the Grand Army, together with a large number of citizens united in doing honor to his memory. "New Hampshire in the Revolution."

SAMUEL SAWINE served in the Massachusetts troops from September 4, 1778, to September 11th, under Capt. John Walter. He came to Kane county, Illinois, and there applied for a pension. "Massachusetts Soldiers in the Revolution."

FREDERICK VAUGHN was born in Connecticut in 1767. He enlisted under Lt. Col. Samuel Canfield in the Connecticut Militia. He came to Kane county, Illinois, and died there August 6, 1845, and was buried in the Root Street cemetery, but through the efforts of the Aurora Chapter, D. A. R., his remains were removed to Spring Lake cemetery, Aurora. The chapter placed a granite and bronze marker at his grave. "Connecticut in the Revolution."

Kendall County

HENRY MIZNER, born in Berks county, Pennsylvania, September 22, 1759; he enlisted in a Northumberland county, Pennsylvania, regiment, serving under Capt. Timothy Green for fifteen months. After the war he came to Indiana, where he received a pension for service in the Revolutionary War. He removed to Illinois, settling in Kendall county, where he died September 25, 1848; is buried in the Millington cemetery, Kendall county.

Knox County

ADAM BRUNER was born in Maryland in 1763. He enlisted February 4, 1781, in Capt. John Gayers company, Third regiment, and Major Richard Salter's regiment, Pennsylvania Militia. He removed to Knox county, Illinois, and died there October 19, 1846. He is buried near Rio in the Bruner cemetery. "Pennsylvania Archives."

PETER BRUNER was born in Maryland in 1762. He enlisted in Capt. George Feathers company, Ninth Battalion, Lancaster county Militia, and Col. John Huber's regiment, in 1779. He again served in Capt. John Smuller's company, in 1780 and 1781; again in 1782 in Capt. James Patten's company. He is buried in the Bruner cemetery near Rio. A monument has been erected to the memory of these brothers in Knox county. "Pennsylvania Archives."

ASHAEL GILBERT was born in Hebron, Connecticut, May 6, 1760. He enlisted May 1, 1778, serving as trumpeter in Capt. Israel Seymour's company, second brigade, with Col. Elijah Sheldon's regiment. He was discharged in 1780. He came to Galesburg, Knox county, in 1847, and died there November 23, 1852. His grave is marked. "Connecticut in the Revolution."

ABRAHAM HAPSONSTALL was born April 6, 1761, in Orange county, New York. He served in the war with Capt. Thomas Moffatt for three months in 1775. He again served with Capt. Seth Marvin for three months, and again with Capt. Francis Smith for six months. He removed to Ohio and from there to Knox county, Illinois, where he died February 4, 1858, and is buried in the Russell cemetery, two miles north of Gilson. He was pensioned.

JOHN HARRINGTON was born February 8, 1764, in Poughkeepsie, New York. He enlisted in May, the year Fort Ann was taken, in Capt. Peter Magee's company, and Col. Henry Livingston's regiment, serving until November in the New York line of troops. He came to Knox county, Illinois, and applied for a pension in 1841, but not having served six months, it was not granted. "New York in the Revolution," and "Pension Reports."

JONATHAN LATIMER was from New London, Conn., where he served in the Third regiment, known as Webb's regiment. He was commissioned as Captain, then Major, and finally served as Colonel of his regiment. He was the father of a remarkable family of sons, six of whom served in the war. He came to Knox county, Illinois, in 1832, and died there. He is buried in the Cherry Grove cemetery, near Abingdon. Such men did not stop to ask "what is all this worth, or what is there in it for me?" Rather did they cherish high ideals, and these ideals were placed above all else that the world could give. "Connecticut in the Revolution."

DAVID MANLEY was from Easton, Mass., where he enlisted with Col. Thomas Carpenter, and Capt. Samuel White, in August, 1778, being discharged in September the same year. He came to Knox county to reside and died there; is buried in the Russell cemetery, north of Gilson. "Massachusetts Soldiers and Sailors."

GEORGE SORNBERGER was born in New York, in 1759. He served under Col. Roswell Hopkins in the Dutchess county Militia. He came to Knox county, Illinois, settling in Victoria, where he died September 27, 1841. "New York in the Revolution."

JOHN STRANGE was born in Westchester county, New York. He enlisted from that county under Col. Pierre Van Courtland. He came to Knox county, Illinois, and died there in 1840 aged 94 years. He is buried in the Russell cemetery. "New York in the Revolution."

Lake County

HENRY COLLINS was born in Massachusetts. He enlisted March 3, 1781, in Southboro for three years under Capt. Isaac Newton. He came to Lake county, Illinois, and died at Newport in 1847, aged 84 years. "Massachusetts in the Revolution."

Lawrence County

JAMES BEARD was born in Pennsylvania. He served in the war from Cumberland county in the 2d company, 4th battalion, under Col. Samuel Culbertson, in 1782, and the same year with Capt. John McConnell. He removed to Kentucky and in 1810 came to Lawrence county, Illinois. Soon after the close of the war of 1812 he was plowing in a field when an Indian who had a fancied grievance against him, stole up behind him and shot him, killing him instantly. Thus came the tragic close of a life of service for his country. He was never married. He lies buried near Heathville, Crawford county, but is near the line in Lawrence county. "Pennsylvania Archives" and "County History."

ISHAM CHILDERS was born in Warren county, North Carolina, in 1766. He enlisted in 1779 for three months with Capt. Rowland Blanton and Col. Sewel; he again enlisted for three months with the same officers. In 1781 he served with Capt. William Johnston in the North Caro lina troops. He removed to Lawrence county, Illinois, and died there. He is buried in Allison township, in the Howard graveyard. He was pensioned.

CHRISTOPHER COY was from Maryland, where he was born in 1761. He enlisted in 1779 under Capt. Henry Gaither, and Col. William Smallwood, serving to the close of the war. He was in the siege of Yorktown. He removed to Kentucky and from there to Lawrence county, Illinois, where he died October 12, 1839, and is buried in the Spring Hill cemetery. He was pensioned.

WILLIAM DENISON was probably from Connecticut and served in 1777. He was at Yorktown under Lafayette. He came to Lawrence county, Illinois, where he died and is buried in the Denison graveyard in the town of Denison. "Family Traditions."

TOUSSAINT DUBOIS was born in Vincennes, Indiana, about 1753. In 1774 he settled in what is now Allison township, Lawrence county. When Father Pierre Gibault came to Vincennes at the request of George Rogers Clark to use his influence with the French inhabitants of that place, Toussaint Dubois with his father and many others took the oath of allegiance in the little French church. He was also selected to confer with Washington regarding supplies. He was drowned while crossing the little Wabash river in 1811. "From Records found in St. Francis Xavier's Church, Vincennes."

TRUMAN GIBBS was from Litchfield, Conn. He served as trumpeter in 1776 with Capt. Moses Seymour and Major Elisha Sheldon in the Connecticut militia. He came to Lawrence county, Illinois, and died there and is buried in Bridgeport in the Spring Grove cemetery.

"Revolutionary soldiers buried in Litchfield, Conn.," by Richards.

JOHN GLENN served from Virginia, in the Revolutionary war, and also continued in the service after the close of the war. He came to Lawrence county, Illinois, and is probably buried there. "Virginia Records."

BENJAMIN HIGHSMITH was from New Jersey. He is said to have served in the war, but no official record of service has been obtained. He came to Lawrence county, Illinois, and settled in what is now Montgomery township, where he died in 1832 and is buried near his home. "Family History."

SAMUEL KINCAID, or Kincade, came from New Jersey to Illinois. He settled in Lukin township in 1819. He died soon after coming and is buried in the Kincaid graveyard, Lukin township. "County History."

ADAM LACKEY was born in Baltimore, Md., in 1759. He enlisted in 1777 for three months, again for four months with Capt. William Wallace, and Col. Isaac Shelby in the Virginia line of troops. He served again for three months under Capt. William Welcher, and Col. Evan Shelby. He was in the battle of Monks Corner. He came to Lawrence county, Illinois, in 1815, and died there in 1836, aged 77 years, and is buried in the Lackey cemetery, Russell township. He was pensioned.

THOMAS LUKE served in the Pennsylvania line of troops. He came to Lawrence county and there applied for a pension, but having served less than six months it was not granted. "Pennsylvania Archives."

BENJAMIN MELTON served in the North Carolina troops with Capt. Berry Turner, Col. Henry Dixon, in 1776. He was drafted in 1781, serving three months, with Capt. William Hardin and Major Sharp. He again served for one year with Capt. Tilgham Dixon and Col. Henry Dixon. He came to Lawrence county, Illinois, in 1820, and died there and is buried in the Melton graveyard, in Denison township. He was pensioned.

WILLIAM MELTON also served in the North Carolina troops with Capt. Henry Dixon from December 13, 1776, to February 1, 1780, in the First regiment. He came to Lawrence county and died there. He is buried in the Melton graveyard, in the town of Denison. He was pensioned.

ANDREW PINKSTAFF was born in Frederick county, Virginia. He enlisted under Capt. George Berry, serving six months. He again served at two different times for eighteen months under Col. Daniel Morgan. He was in the battles of Cowpens and Guildford Court House. He came to Lawrence county and died there September 24, 1841, aged 99 years. He is buried in the Pinkstaff graveyard. The family have his sabre and other relics. "Family History."

CHARLES REED served as a cadet in the Virginia line of troops. He came to Lawrence county, Illinois, and there applied for a pension, but had not served the required time. "Pension Reports."

JAMES ROBINSON was born in Pennsylvania in 1761. He enlisted in 1776 under Capt. Andrew Kilbreth and James Waugh, with Cols. Frederick Watts and Anthony Wayne in the Pennsylvania line of troops. He again enlisted in 1778, for two months with Capt. James Lord, and in 1779 he served for ten months with Capt. John Rowan and Capt. Michael Simpson. He was in the battles of Trenton and others also with the Six Nations of Indians. He removed to Lawrence county, Illinois, where he died September 3, 1834. "Pensylvania Archives" and "Pension Reports."

JOHN ROGERS sered in the Virginia troops and continued in the service after the war. He came to Lawrence county, Illinois, and probably died there. "Virginia Records."

WILLIAM SPENCER came from Pennsylvania. He served in the war, probably from that state, but no official record of service has been obtained. In after life he was known as Colonel, and he was Captain of the Militia in Indiana. He came to Illinois at an early date, and died there. He lies buried in the old cemetery in Lawrence township. "Family History."

STEPHEN TERRY served in the war from Virginia, and continued in the service after the close of the war. He came to Lawrence county, and probably died there. "Virginia Records."

JAMES THOMPSON was in the war from Virginia. He served after the close of the war. He came to Lawrence county and is doubtless buried there. "Virginia Records."

Logan County

PETER BORDERS served in the South Carolina troops; was from Newberry county. He came to Sangamon county, but died in Logan county. He applied for a pension. "Pension Records."

HENRY KIMES was born in Chester county, Pennsylvania. He served under Capt. Edward Vernon in the Chester county militia in 1780, also with Capt. James Denning in 1781 and 1782. He came to Illinois, settling in Logan county, where he died, and is buried near Lincoln. His grave has been marked. "Pennsylvania Archives."

HUMPHREY SCROGGIN was from the Carolinas. He served with Capt. S. Tarrant, Major George Waller and Col. Abram Penn. In 1781 his regiment was ordered from Henry county, Virginia, to the assistance of Gen. Edward Stevens and Gen. Nathaniel Greene at the battle of Guildford Court House. He was also at the siege of Yorktown. He came to Logan county, Illinois, and died there; is buried near Mt. Pulaski. He applied for a pension in Sangamon county. "Pension Reports" and "Family History."

JAMES TURLEY served in the war from Virginia in 1777, in Capt. Thomas Pollard's company and Col. Rumsey's regiment. He again enlisted in 1781, and again for four weeks in

Col. Lyon's regiment. He was in the battle of Germantown. He came to Sangamon county to reside, but died in Logan county, and is buried in the Carlyle cemetery, which was at that time known as the Turley graveyard. He was pensioned.

Macon County

WILLIAM DICKEY enlisted when quite young in the Virginia troops, under Capt. William Waters, in the First Artillery Regiment, commanded by Col. Charles Harrison. He served three years. Coming to Illinois in 1829, he settled in Macon county, where he died in 1832, and is buried in the old French Creek cemetery, Argenta. On June 6, 1912, the Decatur Chapter, D. A. R., placed a marker at his grave with impressive ceremonies. Four generations were present. "Virginia Records."

JOHN FRENCH served in the Virginia troops. He came to Macon county to reside and there applied for a pension. "Virginia Records" and "Pension Reports."

Macoupin County

SAMUEL BROWN was from Virginia, where he served in the war. He came to Illinois and lived in Morgan county, but died in Macoupin county. His burial place is not known. He was pensioned.

ROBERT BUSBY was born in Hanover county, Virginia, July, 1759. He served in the Virginia troops. He removed to Morgan county, Illinois, but died in Macoupin county after 1839. He was pensioned.

HURIAH GILMORE was born in North Carolina in 1749. He came to Morgan county, Illinois, but died in Macoupin county. He died very aged. He was pensioned.

JOHN MAYFIELD was from Warren county, Halifax district, North Carolina, where he served in the war. He came to Macoupin county, Illinois, where he applied for a pension. "Pension Reports" and "North Carolina in the Revolution."

THOMAS MOORE was born in Rockingham county, Virginia, January 24, 1760. He served under Capt. Peter May and Col. John Glenn. He removed to Kentucky, and in 1831 came to Macoupin county, Illinois, where he died, and is buried on the land entered by him and his brother. He is buried in the Moore cemetery. He was pensioned.

JOHN PEEBLES was born about 1762. He early enlisted in the service. In 1847 he made affidavit that he had served under Capt. William Nettles in Gen. Francis Marion's army. He was in the battles of Eutaw Springs and in North Carolina in the "Truce Lands," also in scouting parties. He removed to Kentucky, and later to Macoupin county, Illinois, where he died October 6, 1849. He is buried in the cemetery near Chesterfield. A monument marks his grave. "Family Records" and "Pension Reports."

JOSHUA RICHARDSON was born in Virginia December 19, 1762, in Bedford county. He served in the Virginia troops. He came to Macoupin county, Illinois, and died there March 4, 1844. He was pensioned.

JOHN ROBINSON was from North Carolina, where he served in the war as a musician in the Tenth Regiment under Capt. Thomas

Evans. He enlisted for eighteen months in 1782. He came to Morgan county, Illinois, but died in Macoupin county. He was pensioned.

REUBEN ROSS was born in Harvord, Maryland, in 1756. He enlisted July 30, 1776, in Capt. Alexander Lawson Smith's company and in Col. Moses Rawling's Fourth Regiment, commanded by Col. J. C. Hall. He removed to North Carolina, and then to Morgan county, Illinois. In 1829 he settled in South Palmyra township, section 8, which is now in Macoupin county, where he died. "Maryland in the Revolution" and "Pension Reports."

Madison County

Illinois cannot claim the length of years in the settlement of towns and cities of some eastern states, yet long before Vermont and Kentucky (the first states admitted to the Union after the close of the Revolutionary War) were heard of, the Illinois country occupied a place on the maps of North America, and were Kaskaskia not submerged by the Mississippi river, Illinois could proudly boast of that early settlement, the capital of the Illinois country for seventy-eight years, and afterward of the state.

The centennial mark of one of the counties was reached on September 14, 1912. Appreciating this honor of one hundred years of organization, the citizens of Madison county united in a grand celebration lasting from September 14 to 21, inclusive.

It was a time for the home-coming of former residents, who vied with each other and with those now living in the county in making the centennial celebration a marked event not only for the county but for Edwardsville, the county seat.

Madison county was created a separate county by proclamation of Governor Ninian Edwards in September, 1812; it was fitting, therefore, that the State Legislature should appropriate $5,000.00 for the erection of a monument in Edwardsville to commemorate a century of progress in the county and in memory of Gov. Edwards and those whose life work was given in aid of the development of Madison county. On September 16, 1912, the monument was dedicated with elaborate and fitting ceremonies.

This historic day closed with the unveiling of a bronze tablet in the circuit court room of the court house at Edwardsville in memory of the Revolutionary soldiers who lie buried in Madison county.

Thus were linked together in history the two wars for independence, as well as the part taken by these pioneer-patriots who aided in laying the foundations for the successful development of Madison county.

The program was in charge of the Ninian Edwards Chapter of the D. A. R., of Alton, who, with descendants of the men, placed the tablet in grateful recognition of service rendered by these soldiers, who with their compatriots were the most heroic, the most devoted to duty of all men, ancient or modern.

The program opened with an invocation by Rev. J. W. McNeill; Hon. Norman G. Flagg gave an appropriate introductory address; Gov. Charles S. Deneen, whose native city is Edwardsville, brought greetings from the state of Illinois, giving praise to the D. A. R. for their historic-patriotic work, expressing the hope that every county in the state where Revolutionary soldiers are buried would place a marker, either in bronze or stone, to their memory.

Grandmother's Story of Bunker Hill was read by Miss Nina Gaskins, a lineal descendant of William McAdams, whose name is engraved on the tablet. Mrs. L. M. Castle, regent of the Ninian Edwards Chapter of Alton, the youngest chapter in the state, presented the tablet to the county, in eloquent words portraying the life of the soldiers of the Revolution, not forgetting the part taken by the women of that period.

The tablet was unveiled by Master Norman F. Gillham, who has the honor of being descended from Gaius Paddock and John Gillham, two soldiers, who were honored by their names being placed in lasting remembrance, also he can claim ten direct ancestors, in addition to those already mentioned, who rendered service in the Revolutionary War; also by Master William Krome Delicate, a descendant of Thomas Gillham, one of four by the name of Gillham, all brothers, whose names are engraved on bronze.

The acceptance of the tablet was appropriately assigned to Hon. William H. Hall, a direct descendant of William Hall.

ABSALOM BAKER was a native of North Carolina, where he enlisted in May, 1775, under Capt. John Brannon, serving until 1781. He was in the battles of Stono and Bacon's (Biggin's) Bridge; was taken prisoner at the siege of Charleston and held thirty days; was in Buford's defeat, the battle of Ramsour's Mills, Sumter's defeat at Hanging Rock; was wounded in the battle of Gates' defeat near Camden, and was in the battle of King's Mountain, Monk's

Corner, Guilford Court House and Eutaw Springs. A remarkable record for one man. He came to Illinois in 1824, settling in Sangamon county, but removed to Madison county, where he died in 1833. He was pensioned.

WILLIAM BIGGS was born in Maryland in 1755. He enlisted with George Rogers Clark for the conquest of Illinois and was made lieutenant of his company. Returning to Virginia, he decided to make Illinois his home, removing there in 1784, settling near Bellefontaine, Monroe county. He was twice elected to represent Illinois territory at Vincennes, 1812-1814. Later he was elected senator. In 1789 he was captured by the Kickapoo Indians, but was released by paying a heavy ransom. He removed to Madison county and died in 1827 at the residence of Major Samuel Judy, and is buried in Madison county, six miles south of Edwardsville, at Peters Station.

GEORGE BRIDGES, a native of North Carolina, born February 12, 1762, near Elizabeth, on Cape Fear river. He enlisted at Salisbury March 10, 1777, under Capts. Griffith McCrea and Christopher Goodwin, serving nineteen months; enlisted again June, 1780, for three months under Capt. James Craig and Col. John Fifer; he again enlisted November, 1780, for three months, again serving for three months when he was taken prisoner by the British; and finally for another term of three months in May, 1781. This record covers five terms of service during the war; for a time he acted as drummer for his company. Coming to Madison county, Illinois, in 1808, he settled near Troy. He applied for a pension in 1832, which was granted.

DANIEL BROWN was born October, 1757, in Bucks county, Pennsylvania. Removing to Virginia, he enlisted in Augusta county August 8, 1776, under Capt. John Gilmore., Cols. William Russell and William Christian, serving three months; enlisted again for six weeks under Capt. Charles Gadliff; again for six weeks under Capt. John Martin; again for one month from May, 1782, was made sergeant under Capt. Robert McBride, Col. Stephen Trigg, and October, 1782, he served for one month under Capt. Samuel Kirkham, Col. Benjamin Logan. Daniel Brown showed his patriotism by re-enlisting after the war in 1786 for a short term of service. His claim for a pension was allowed in 1832, at which time he resided in Madison county, Illinois, where he lies buried in the Wanda cemetery.

JOHN CARNELISON was a native of North Carolina. He enlisted June, 1778, under Capts. John Armstrong and Matthew Ramsey, Cols. Robert Mebane, Archibald Lytle and John McLean; he again enlisted for four years under Capts. Smith, Adolph Hedrick, Francis Cole, John Childs and Jennings. He was in the battle of Stono. His claim for a pension was allowed while a resident of Fayette county, Kentucky. Removing to Illinois, he settled in Greene county, then in Madison county, where he lived with Solomon Pruit in 1840. He was 82 years of age and resided with W. C. Johns.

MICHAEL DECK was born in Rockingham county, Virginia, in 1759, where he married, April 25, 1790, Susanna Monger, who was born April 10, 1759. He died April 13, 1843, and his widow was allowed his pension. Michael Deck enlisted May 5, 1778, under Capt. Robert

Craven, and again in 1781 under Capt. Michael Coker. He was in the battle of Yorktown. He early came to Madison county to reside, and is buried in Marine. He left a large family of children, thirteen in number.

THE GILLHAMS. Seldom do we read of so remarkable a family record for enthusiastic patriotic service as the war record of the Gillham family. Thomas Gillham came to America from Ireland in 1730, settling first in Virginia. He removed to South Carolina, Pendleton county. He early espoused the cause of the Colonies, and with his seven sons and two sons-in-law served in the Revolutionary War. Five of these sons came to Madison county to reside, one, William, later removed to Jersey county. Four names are engraved upon the bronze tablet; only two ever applied for pensions.

ISAAC GILLHAM was born in Augusta county, Virginia, November 10, 1757; removed to South Carolina in 1763; enlisted in Camden district December, 1777, for fifty days under Capt. Robert Macupfee, Col. Thomas Neel; again March 29, 1778, under Lieut. Thomas Gillham (probably his father), when he was wounded; served again from May, 1780, to August 18, 1780, under Capt. Jacob Barnett and Col. Thomas Neel; again enlisting February 15, 1781, to May 1, 1781; again serving as a scout during the winter and spring of 1781 and 1782, with Capt. Jacob Barnett, Col. William Bratton and Major John Hartshorn. Isaac Gillham was engaged in the battles of Rocky Mount and Fishing Creek. He early came to Madison county, Illinois, where his claim for a pension was allowed.

JAMES GILLHAM, a son of Thomas, also served with his father and brothers in the war, enlisting in South Carolina, serving acceptably always, then joining the family came to Illinois, settling in Madison county, where he lies buried. He married Anne Barnett, sister of Capt. Barnett, under whom he served. "Family History."

THOMAS GILLHAM, the third son of Thomas, served 210 days in Capt. Jacob Barnett's company, William Hill's regiment, and fourteen days in Capt. James Thompson's company, William Bratton's regiment, and forty days in the same company under Lieut. Dervin, and for this service was paid by the state treasurer. Thomas Gillham came to Madison county with his brothers. "South Carolina Records."

JOHN GILLHAM, the fourth son of Thomas, Sr., served in the Sixth South Carolina Regiment as corporal; enlisting March 23, 1776; was discharged June 1, 1777; he was also in the militia under Col. Thomas Brandon. John Gillham married Sarah Clark in South Carolina and with other pioneers they came to Illinois, settling on the west bank of Cahokia creek in 1802, in the month of June. He died March, 1832, and is buried with his three brothers in the Wanda cemetery. "South Carolina Records" and "Family History."

WILLIAM HALL, a native of Pennsylvania, born in 1762, near Lancaster. He removed to South Carolina and did valiant service in the war of the Revolution. Enlisted in April, 1779, at Long Cane, South Carolina, taking the place of his uncle, William; marched to Savannah, Georgia, which was burned, later joining Gen. Benjamin Lincoln at St. Marys; served under

Capt. James McCall; was made sergeant in Capt. William Alexander's company, serving four months. After serving a similar period in Capt. Gilbert Falls' company he was transferred to Capt. James Duckworth's company, where he served three months. He aided in the defense of Charleston, then entered Capt. John Pitt's company, was detailed to transfer provisions to Gen. Horatio Gates until the battle of Camden, August, 1780; during his fifth service under Capt. Falls, who was killed in this battle, he was in the battles of Ramsour Mills and Guilford Court House; was also in the battle of Eutaw Springs, where he had charge of seventy-five prisoners captured in that engagement and delivered them to Gen. Francis Locke. William Hall lived in North Carolina and Tennessee, and in 1815 he removed to Madison county, Illinois, settling near Collinsville. He died May 13, 1846. A government marker has been placed on his grave. "South Carolina Records."

ANTHONY A. HARRISON was born March 18, 1763, in Westmoreland county, Virginia. He enlisted in Greenville county, Virginia, February, 1781, serving five months under Capt. John Lucas, re-enlisted for six weeks under Capt. Benjamin Newson; he again enlisted in his brother's company, Capt. Joseph Harrison, Col. Alexander Dick. He was in the battle of Petersburg; he applied for a pension while living in Greenfield township, Madison county. He died in 1842, and is buried in Madison county. He was pensioned.

SAMUEL HUDSON was from Middlesex county, New Jersey, where he enlisted for service. He came to Madison county, Illinois, and there applied for a pension. "New Jersey in the Revolution."

BENJAMIN JOHNSON was a native of Orange county, Virginia, born in 1758. He served in the Revolutionary War from that state and received a pension for his service. While a resident of Virginia he is said to have held eighteen slaves. After the war he removed to Madison county, and was living in 1840, aged 82. The exact place of his burial is not known. He lived with W. L. Harrison.

JOHN LONG, a native of North Carolina, born in 1732 in Granville; died in Madison county February 10, 1839. He enlisted at Granville, serving three months under Capt. James Pearce, March 1, 1781, and three months from August 1, 1781, under Capt. Hargron Searsay, Col. Thomas Taylor. He was in the battle of Guilford Court House. John Long married in Caswell county, North Carolina, Frances Estes; they came to Madison county, Illinois, at an early day and prospered financially, owning large tracts of land, and after the custom of those early days they kept a hotel. He was pensioned.

ELIHU MATHER, as the name indicates, was a resident of Connecticut, from Windsor, where he enlisted in the Third Regiment under Col. Samuel Wyllys, in Capt. Daniel Allin's company; he was a sergeant in the Fourth Regiment under Col. Zebulon Butler January 1, 1781. He came to Illinois at an early day, settling in Madison county, where he died and lies buried, probably in Collinsville. "Connecticut in the Revolution."

WILLIAM McADAMS was born in York county, Pennsylvania, in 1760. He enlisted at Hawsfield, Orange county, North Carolina, in the spring of 1779, for three months, under Capt. John Carrington, Col. Martin Armstrong, enlisting again for two years, from 1780 to 1782, under Capt. William Douglass and Nathaniel Christman, Col. William O'Neale. After he came to Madison county, Illinois, to reside he applied for a pension, which was granted. He is probably buried in Jarvis. He was pensioned.

GAIUS PADDOCK, a native of Massachusetts, enlisted in the conflict; was a member of Capt. Isaac Wood's company, Col. William Larned's regiment. He entered the service January 1, 1776; was afterward with the troops that evacuated New York; was in the battle of Trenton and the skirmish at Frog Neck. He re-enlisted for six weeks and was in the second battle of Trenton and of Princeton; was in several skirmishes, and in 1779 and 1780 he served under Lieut. Joseph Bates, Col. Gamaliel Bradford's regiment, Massachusetts line of troops. Coming west, he located in Madison county, and lies buried in the family burying ground near Moro. "Massachusetts in the Revolution."

GEORGE PRICKETT was a native of Maryland, where he probably served in the war. He removed to one of the Carolinas, and from there to Georgia, then to Kentucky, and in 1808 came to Madison county, Illinois, where he died in 1846. He is buried in Woodlawn cemetery, Edwardsville. "County History."

MARTIN PRUIT was born in Virginia in 1748. He enlisted in the fall of 1778 for two years under Capts. William Campbell and William Edminton with Col. William Campbell, who was made colonel in 1780. He served as sergeant. He was in the battle of King's Mountain. He came to Illinois in 1806 and resided in

Madison county, where he died, and lies buried in the family burying ground in Fort Russell. He applied for a pension in 1832 at the age of 84 years. He died in 1844, aged 92 years.

ISHAM RANDLE was a native of Brunswick county, Virginia, born in 1759. He removed to North Carolina, where he enlisted in Montgomery county, but later he re-enlisted in Brunswick county, Virginia. His first service was in 1780, for three months under Capt. Abner Crump, Col. Dowy Leadbetter. The second service was November, 1781, for four months with Capt. Edmund Wilkins. He applied for a pension while a resident of Goshen, Madison county, in 1832. It is not known where he is buried.

RICHARD RANDLE was born in Brunswick county, Virginia, in 1751. He was doubtless a brother of Isham. He enlisted in Brunswick county in 1777 for six weeks with Capt. John Macklin, Col. Charles Harrison, Virginia line of troops; he again enlisted August, 1780, for nine months with Capts. James Allen and West Harris in the North Carolina troops. With his younger brother he came to Madison county, Illinois, to reside, where he died at an advanced age. He and Isham are doubtless buried in Goshen. He was pensioned.

HENRY REVIS was born August 11, 1752, in Northampton county, North Carolina. He enlisted in the fall of 1775 for three months with Capt. Jacob Free; re-enlisted for three months under the same officer; enlisted again under Capt. William Neville, Col. Martin Armstrong. His entire service was for one year. He enlisted at Surry county, North Carolina. He came to Illinois with his brother and resided in Madison county, where he died; is probably buried in Collinsville. Was pensioned in 1832.

WILLIAM RICHARDS served in the Virginia line of troops and he also continued in the service of the United States troops after the war. He came to reside in Madison county, Illinois, where he is doubtless buried. "Virginia Records."

FRANCIS ROACH was born in Fairfax county, Virginia, in 1739. He removed to North Carolina, where he enlisted in Dobbs county April, 1776, in Joseph Session's company, Col. Richard Caswell and Col. John Bryant; enlisted again for three months in 1781 under Capt. John Doughty; re-enlisted in 1782 for two months under Col. George Rogers Clark; he again served his country by enlisting in the militia in 1786 under Capt. John Doughty and Col. Benjamin Logan. He came to Madison county to reside and his claim for a pension was allowed in 1832. Francis Roach located in Hamel, where he died in 1845 at the advanced age of 106 years.

LABAN SMART, a native of North Carolina, born November 9, 1759, in Franklin county. He enlisted early in 1780 for three months under Capt. William Brickle, Cols. Allen, Sessions and Kinyon; re-enlisted in 1781 for three months under Capt. Daniel Jones, Col. William Linton. There is no record of any battles in which he was engaged. He came to Illinois and settled in Pin Oak township, Madison county, where descendants of his still live. He was pensioned in 1832.

HENRY THORNHILL was born in Virginia in 1757. He entered the service in Rockingham county under Capt. Robert Craven, the year he could not remember, and served six months; again enlisted, serving under Capt. Daniel Ragan, Tenth Virginia Regiment, for three months, and was discharged at Yorktown, five days before the surrender of Lord Cornwallis. In 1832 he was allowed a pension while a resident of Goshen, Madison county, where he is doubtless buried.

JABEZ TURNER was a "Revolutionist before the Revolution," since he entered the service in May, 1775, serving six months as private under Capt. Samuel Wilmot in Col. Andrew Ward's regiment, Connecticut line of troops; again for six weeks in 1776 with Capt. Caleb Allen, Col. Jabez Thompson; again in December, 1776, for three weeks under Capt. Peter Johnson; again for ten days in April, 1777, under Capt. Caleb Mix, and the fifth time he enlisted October, 1777, for two weeks with Capt. James Hillhouse. He was engaged in the expedition to St. Johns and Montreal; he was serving when the British threatened New York, and retreated with his regiment from Long Island; was actively engaged when the entrance of the British into New Haven was resisted. Jabez Turner was born in New Haven, Connecticut, January 31, 1756, and died in Godfrey, Madison county, Illinois, December 12, 1846, when past 90 years of age. He removed to Great Barrington, Massachusetts, and later to Columbia county, New York, and a few years later came to Madison county, Illinois, to reside. Several years ago his grave was marked with impressive ceremonies, the teachers and pupils of the public schools were in attendance, thus an object lesson in patriotic study was given at the grave of this hero. "Connecticut in the Revolution."

Marion County

THOMAS ASHE was from North Carolina, where he served in the war. He came to Marion county, Illinois, before 1825, and in 1833 applied for a pension. His place of burial is not known. "County History."

SAMUEL EBELIN was born in 1755 in Virginia. He enlisted in Loudoun county in 1777 for three months with Capt. John Henry; again in June, 1781, for three months under Capt. Thomas Cowan and Major Jeremiah Risley, Virginia troops. He was in the second battle of Stillwater. He removed to Marion county, Illinois, and died there. He was pensioned.

PETER FINN was born July 2, 1751, in Baltimore county, Maryland. He enlisted in 1778 under Capt. John Murray for nine months, and Col. Archibald Thompson, Maryland troops. He again enlisted in North Carolina in 1779 with Capt. Valentine Sevier (Col. Benjamin Carter, and Col. Charles Robertson). He again served as Sergeant in 1780 for three months with Capt. Valentine Sevier, and Col. John Sevier, North Carolina troops. He removed to Kentucky and from there applied for a pension. He came to Marion county, Illinois, in 1837, and died there. He was pensioned.

WILLIAM GASTON was born in South Carolina, and served in the war from that state. He enlisted five times; first in 1775 for two months, again in 1776 for one year and four teen days, and again he served for two months the same year. He again served in 1780 for one year, and in 1781 for one year with Capts. Thomas Marshall, John McClure, and John Steele. He was in several battles, notably King's Mountain, Hooks Defeat, and Hanging Rock. He early came to Illinois, settling at "Devil's Bake Oven" in 1814. He is said to have been a great singer. He died in Marion county and is buried in a country cemetery near a church at Walnut Hills. On his monument is inscribed, "Served under Washington." He was pensioned.

MICHAEL LUTTRELL was born in Virginia, October, 1751, in Fauquier county. He served in 1781 under Capt. George Shelton and Col. William Churchill; again the same year with Capt. Thomas Helm and Major John Chun in the Virginia troops. He removed to Illinois, settling in Marion county, near Salem; later in Iuka township. He died December 19, 1844, and was doubtless buried near Iuka. He was pensioned.

JOSEPH MORRISON was born November 30, 1759, in Martinsburg, Berkeley county, Virginia. He was drafted and served nine months in 1776 under Capts. John Lyle, Anthony Odel, and Jacob Linder, with Cols. John Morrow and William Morgan. He aided in erecting Fort McIntosh, and was at the surrender of Yorktown. He came to Marion county, Illinois, and died there August 23, 1835. His widow, Elizabeth, drew a pension after his death. He was pensioned.

GEORGE ROPER was from North Carolina and served in the war from that state under Capt. Anthony Sharp, in the Tenth Regiment, and was discharged April 15, 1782. He removed to Illinois, residing in Clinton county, and later in Jefferson county, but died in Marion county. He was pensioned.

SAMUEL YOUNG was born May 7, 1762, in Cumberland county, Pennsylvania. He enlisted first in Northumberland county, Pennsylvania, May 7, 1778, for three months with Capt. Samuel Young and Col. Dougherty in the Pennsylvania troops. He enlisted again in 1781 for three months with Capt. James Montgomery and Col. William Campbell in the Virginia troops, and again in 1782 for three months with the same officers. After the war he removed to Rowan county, North Carolina; then to Rutherford county, then Spartanburg county, South Carolina; then to Franklin county, Georgia; then to Sumner county, Tennessee; then to Logan county, Kentucky; then to Indiana, and finally to Gallatin county, Illinois, and later to Marion county, where he died in 1846. He was buried in the Young graveyard. Later in life he was called Captain. He was pensioned.

Marshall County

LEMUEL GAYLORD was born February 14, 1765, in Bristol county, Connecticut; died November 17, 1854, and is buried in Cumberland cemetery, Evans township, Marshall county, Illinois. Lemuel Gaylord's father was killed in the famous massacre of Wyoming, July, 1778. His mother at once started for her old home in Connecticut, suffering untold hardships on the way. Three years after her return, Lemuel enlisted, serving as ensign in Col. Roger Enos' company. After the war he removed to Illinois, settling in what is now Marshall county. Kathryn Gaylord, his mother, was the first Revolutionary heroine, for whom a public monument was erected, and the Bristol Chapter, D. A. R., of Connecticut, is named in honor of Kathryn Gaylord, the mother of this hero of the American Revolution. "Connecticut in the Revolution."

JOSEPH WARNER was born in Anne Arundel county, Maryland, March, 1738; he removed to Fairfax county, Virginia, and enlisted from there; was in the battle of Germantown, 1779. In 1802 he removed to Ohio, and in 1838, at the advanced age of 100 years, he came to Illinois, coming the entire distance on horse-back, residing at Cherry Point, Marshall county. He longed for his old home in Ohio, and when 102 years of age, he started back, walking twelve miles across the unbroken prairie, where friends gave him shelter and persuaded him to return to Cherry Point.

Another incident illustrating the indomitable courage and zeal, both Christian and patriotic, with which these pioneer-patriots were endowed: One cold, sleety Sunday, his daughter thought Mr. Warner ought not to attend church, but fearing he would be left at home, he started on foot. There was a creek to be crossed which he did by lying down and crawling over on two icy poles. This when he was 102 years of age. The aged pariot died September 5, 1842, and lies buried in Cherry Point, where a monument marks his last resting place. "Virginia" and "Family Records."

Mason County

WILLIAM LANGSTON served in the war from Virginia. He removed to North Carolina, living in Wayne county. He was wounded in the hand. He came to Coles county, Illinois, but died in Mason county November, 1835, aged 93 years. He is buried six miles east of Manito. A marble slab marks his grave. "Virginia" and "Family Records."

McDonough County

JONAS HOBART was born in New Hampshire November 15, 1744. His brother, Isaac, was killed at the battle of Bunker Hill; hearing of his death, Jonas determined to enter the service and enlisted March 17, 1777, serving as corporal in the Fourth Company, First Regiment, New Hampshire troops. He was in the battle of Ticonderoga, where he was wounded, a bullet striking his cheek, knocking out two teeth and finally lodging against his left collar bone. This was removed by the use of a pocket knife. The bullet and one tooth are preserved by a descendant. He was discharged January 1, 1781. Coming to Illinois, he lived for a time in Schuyler county, but removed to McDonough county, where he died November, 1833, and is buried in the Foster cemetery, Eldorado township. He was pensioned.

MOSES JUSTUS was born in Maryland in 1755. He enlisted in Mecklenburg county, North Carolina, serving as a "Minute Man" under Capt. John Fifer, July, 1775; again in June, 1779, and in February, 1781, under Capts. Samuel Patton, Caleb Fifer and James Newell, with Cols. John Fifer and Tinnon. He was in the battles of Stono and Wetzell's Mills. Coming to Illinois, he settled in Schuyler county, but removed to McDonough county, where he died at an advanced age. He was pensioned.

WILLIAM WILLARD was born in Loudoun county, Virginia, in 1755; he entered the service in July, 1778, serving under Capt. James Ratekin and Col. Abraham Shepherd. Later he served with Capt. William Douglass and Col. William Russell. He first resided in Morgan county, Illinois, but died in Emmet township, McDonough county, near Colchester, November 9, 1846. He was pensioned.

McLean County

Has preserved in bronze and stone the name of every soldier and sailor who ever resided in the county who participated in any war in which the United States has been engaged. On Memorial Day, May 30, 1913, the monument was dedicated with fitting ceremonies. Twelve names of Revolutionary soldiers who lie buried in McLean county are engraved on the monument. The work of locating the graves and verifying the records of these soldiers was accomplished by Mrs. H. M. Rollins, historian of the Letitia Green Stevenson Chapter, D. A. R., ably assisted by Milo Custer, Esq., who is adding to this accredited list the names and records of Revolutionary soldiers buried in counties adjoining McLean. The spirit of gratitude towards soldiers of any war needs fostering. "Lest we forget; lest we forget."

EBENEZER BARNES was born in Boston, Massachusetts, February 3, 1759; he served his country by enlisting five different times, first as corporal in 1775 under Capt. Archelaus Batchelder, Col. Joseph Read; later the same year as sergeant with Capt. Aldrich; again in 1776 for nine months as sergeant under Capt. Gideon Foster, Col. Ebenezer Smith; re-enlisting in 1777, he was made lieutenant with Capt. Samuel Fletcher, Col. Timothy Bedel's regiment, serving four months; finally, the following summer, 1778, he served ten months as lieutenant with Capt. John Tyler, Col. Joseph Fay, all in Massachusetts line of troops. He was in the battle of White Plains, was pensioned.

Ebenezer Barnes came to McLean county, Illinois, in 1829, settling at Barnes' Grove in Danvers township; he died May 17, 1836, and is probably buried in Stout's Grove cemetery.

JOSEPH BARTHOLMEW was a native of New Jersey, born March 15, 1766; was a private in Capt. Jonathan Rowland's company, Tradyffren, Pennsylvania line of troops, in 1780. He settled in Money Creek township in McLean county, Illinois, in 1830; died near Clarksville, Ill., November 2, 1840, and lies buried in Clarksville cemetery.

CAPT. SAMUEL BEELER, a native of Virginia, born about 1760; served in the Virginia line of troops 158 days. He came to Illinois about 1830, settling in McLean county; died there near Twin Grove January 14, 1840, and is buried in East Twin Grove cemetery. "Virginia Records."

PHILIP CROSE was born in Hampshire county, Virginia, 1757; served as private in Captain Daniel Richardson's company for six months, again the following year, 1781, for four months. He enlisted from Hampshire county, was in the battle of Guilford Court House. After the war was over, he removed to Illinois, settling in Shawneetown, Gallatin county, removed to Indiana, where he applied for and received a pension; from there he came to Illinois and settled in McLean county in 1836, in Randolph township, where he died about 1840.

JOHN ELLSWORTH served in the war from New York, enlisting February, 1776, with Capt. John B. Allen and Col. Frederick Weisenfels, in the Fourth New York Regiment. He was in the battles of Bennington and at Moses Kill, also at the surrender of Burgoyne. After having served three years, he deserted, in 1779. He came to McLean county, Illinois. and there applied for a pension, which was refused, even though he returned to the service, but did not serve six months, which would not entitle him to a pension. "New York in the Revolution" and "Pension Reports."

DAVID HAGGARD was born in Albemarle county, Virginia, in 1762; served in the Virginia line of troops, was in the battle of Yorktown. He came to Illinois in 1836, settled in Bloomington, McLean county; died there April 15, 1843. This record is taken from the Haggard Genealogy. He was doubtless a brother of James Haggard, who is buried in Sangamon county and was pensioned. "Virginia Records" and "Family History."

FRANCIS HODGE was born about 1760. He served in the New Jersey Continental army, in the Artillery commanded by —— Harrison. He came to McLean county, Illinois, and died there about 1836, and is buried in the Frankeberger cemetery. "New Jersey Muster Roll."

MOSES HOUGHAM or HUFFMAN, was a soldier of the American Revolution, serving in the Virginia line of troops. He received his pay at the close of the war at Pittsburg, Pennsylvania. Moses Hougham came to McLean county, Illinois, about 1830, died in 1845, aged 101 years, and is buried in Scogin's cemetery, Bloomington township. "Virginia Records."

CAPTAIN JOHN C. KARR was born in Bucks county, Pennsylvania, 1758; served as captain in Second Battalion, Somerset county, New Jersey, line of troops. He settled in McLean county, Illinois, in 1839; died near Leroy December 16, 1840; buried in Heyworth cemetery. Capt. Karr left in a will the inscription to be placed on his tomb-stone:" Sacred to the Memory of John Karr, a Soldier of the Revolution in 1776." He left a request that he be buried with the honors of war, which request was complied with. He was pensioned.

THOMAS McCLURE was born in Rockingham county, Virginia, July 15, 1765. He was of Scotch-Irish parentage. In 1781 he removed to Kentucky and there aided in fighting the Indians. His brother Robert was killed by the Indians. Coming to Illinois, he settled at Stout's Grove, McLean county, in 1827, and died there January 3, 1847; is buried in Stout's Grove cemetery, Danvers township. His grave is marked with an old soft marble headstone. "County History."

WILLIAM McCULLOUGH was born in Baltimore, Maryland, in 1756. He served as private in Capt. Alexander Lawson Smith's company, Col. Moses Rawling's regiment, Maryland troops, for two years. He came to McLean county, Illinois, about 1830, died there November 23, 1832, and is buried in the old McCullough family cemetery on what is now the Elkins farm. "Maryland in the Revolution."

WILLIAM McGHEE was born in Louisa county, Virginia, in 1761. He was a private, serving five different times in Capt. Pond's company, Col. Wade's regiment; also in Capt. Bracken's company, Col. Lofton's regiment; also in Capt. Smith's company, Col. William Shepard's regiment; also in Capt. John Armstrong's company, Col. Nicholas Lewis' regiment; again in Capt. James Shepard's company, Col. Nicholas Lewis' regiment, all in the North Carolina line of troops. He enlisted from Mecklenburg; was in the battle of Wilmington. He came to McLean county, Illinois, in 1828, and died at Diamond Grove, and is buried there. He died October 6, 1843. He was pensioned.

JOHN TOLIDAY was born near Poughkeepsie, New York, October, 1763. He served in Capt. Samul Bowman's company of New York rangers for four months, again serving under Capt. James Harrison, Col. Lewis Du Bois' regiment, for six months. He came to McLean county, Illinois, in 1830, residing in Mount Hope township. He died in Leroy about 1849, and is buried in Oak Grove cemetery. "New York in the Revolution."

JACOB WILLIAMSON was a soldier in the war, probably serving in the New Jersey line of troops. Mr. William Hieronymus, Jr., an aged resident of McLean county, remembers hearing Jacob Williamson tell of his service in the war. He came to Illinois, settling at Hittle's Grove about 1826. He died in what is now Danvers township, McLean county, June, 1838, and is doubtless buried in Stout's Grove cemetery. "County History" and "Traditional Records."

Menard County

LEWIS FERGUSON was born in Virginia in 1760. He enlisted in Culpeper county in 1778, serving until 1780. He was made lieutenant under Capt. Garland Burrly and Col. Francis Taylor. He died in Menard county in 1842. He was pensioned.

AARON HOUGHTON was born in Hopewell, Hunterdon county, New Jersey, April 15, 1761. He enlisted June, 1776, serving until April, 1777, in his father's company, Capt. Joab Houghton, and Col. James Johnson's regiment. In the fall of the same year he served one month in Lieut. Williams Parks' company, Col. Joab Houghton's regiment. He removed to Kentucky, and from there to Sangamon county, Illinois, in 1824. He died in Menard county in Rock Creek precinct. He was pensioned.

ZACHARIAH NANCE enlisted in New Kent county, Virginia, in Col. Charles Harrison's regiment. He was in the battles of Monmouth and Stony Point. He died in Sangamon county, Illinois, December 22, 1835, but Menard county was set apart from Sangamon in 1839, and the place of burial is now in Menard county. He was pensioned.

JOHN OVERSTREET was born in Virginia, where he enlisted in the First Virginia Cavalry when only fifteen years of age. He enlisted again in 1777 for three years in the Fourteenth Regiment. He was in many battles: Monmouth, Stony Point, Brandywine and Germantown, and was in the siege of Yorktown. He endured great hardships at Valley Forge. He removed to Ohio, and from there to Sangamon county, Illinois, where he died in Fancy Creek township, but was buried across the line in Athens, Menard county. He was buried with military honors. He was pensioned.

JOSHUA SHORT was born in Virginia about 1752. He enlisted in 1776, serving until 1778. At the close of the war he came to Sangamon county, Illinois. He was one of the aged men who rode in a canoe mounted on wheels and rigged as a ship in the procession at the Whig gathering in 1840. He died in Menard county in 1842. "Virginia Records" and "Family History."

JAMES THOMAS was born in Maryland in 1750; enlisted in 1776, serving six years as a private in Capts. David Hopkins and David Plunkett's companies, Col. Stephen Mayland, in Fourth Continental Dragoons. He was wounded in the battles of Germantown and Savannah, was also in the battles of Brandywine, Monmouth and the siege of Yorktown. After the war he removed to Indiana. Coming to Illinois, he resided in Menard county, where he died in 1833. He was pensioned.

BENJAMIN WALKER was born in Pennsylvania in 1758, and died in Menard county in 1847. He served at various times in the Pennsylvania troops from June 1, 1776, to March, 1779. He was given a pension. He died in Menard county, Illinois.

Mercer County

ABNER WATSON was born in Virginia, May, 1754. He enlisted August, 1781, serving until the latter part of September under Capt. Robert Stubblefield and Col. William Dark. He was in the battle of York, Virginia. He removed to Illinois, settling in Shelby county, but died in Mercer county. He was buried in the timber on his farm but later was removed to the cemetery in Riviola. "Pension Reports" and "Family History."

Monroe County

ZEBEDIAH BARKER was born in Methuen, Essex county, Massachusetts. He served as a "Minute Man" and also from June, 1776, for over two years; during this time he was an orderly sergeant under Capt. Maloon, Capt. David Whittier and Col. Thomas Poor. He was in the battle of Stillwater. He came to Illinois in 1818, settling in New Design, Monroe county, where he died October 10, 1819, and was buried on his farm, which is located one and one-half miles from Burkville. He was pensioned.

SHADRACH BOND, SR., was born near Baltimore, Maryland. He came west with George Rogers Clark, being sergeant of his company. In 1781 he returned to Illinois. Before leaving Virginia, in conversation with Hosea Briggs, he remarked that they might represent the Illinois country in the Legislature. Shadrach Bond was a member of the first General Assembly of the territory which convened west of the Ohio river after the Revolutionary War, and served four times; was also elected justice of St. Clair county. He is buried in the old graveyard on the bluff above his residence. He was the uncle of the Shadrach Bond who was the first governor of the state of Illinois. "County History."

EBENEZER BOURN was born in Lebanon, Connecticut, in 1753. He was on an exploring and hunting expedition on the Ohio river when he enlisted under Col. George Rogers Clark in 1778 for fourteen days, Capt. William Harrod Col. George Rogers Clark. He again enlisted for fourteen months with Capt. John Williams, Col.

Montgomery, and Col. William Lynn. He died August 29, 1839, in Harrisonville, Monroe county. He was pensioned.

JAMES GARRETSON was one of Clark's soldiers. Returning to Virginia, he came back to Illinois in 1781, settling near Waterloo, and later in Moredock, where he died.

PIERE GIRADOT was one who greatly aided the American cause. He was made commandant of St. Phillippe and served as justice. He died before 1783 as his widow is given as the head of the family in 1783. "County History."

ANDREW HILTON was a native of Maryland, born in Charles county in 1757. He served three months with Capt. Charles Mills and Col. Hawkins; again enlisting for six months under Capt. Henry Bowman, Col. Hawkins. He came to Illinois, settling in Monroe county, where he drew a pension. He died in Monroe county.

WILLIAM HOWARD served in the war from Virginia. He also continued in the service of his country after the close of the war. He came to Monroe county, Illinois, and probably died there. "Virginia Records" and "Pension Report."

ROBERT KIDD took part in the capture of Fort Gage under Clark. He settled in Monroe county in 1781 in Renault township, and died there in 1849.

JAMES LEMAN was born in Berkeley county, Virginia, in 1760. He enlisted in 1777, was in the battle of White Plains, serving two years. He came to Illinois, settling in New Design, Monroe county, which place he founded. His house, built of brick, is still standing and near the home is the old cemetery where he is buried. He died January 9, 1823. "Virginia Records."

LIEUT. HENRY LEVENS, SR., was from Pennsylvania, but served in the Virginia line of troops. He was born March 26, 1740. He came to Illinois and resided in Morgan county, but removed to Monroe county and died in February, 1835. "Pennsylvania in the Revolution."

THOMAS LOGUE served in the Pennsylvania line of troops. He came to Monroe county, Illinois, to reside and there applied for a pension. "Pennsylvania Archives."

GEORGE LUNSFORD was born in Virginia June 8, 1762. He was one of the soldiers with Col. George Rogers Clark, who with his command captured Kaskaskia and Prairie du Rocher in 1778. George Lunsford enlisted again January 20, 1780, and was discharged February 18, 1783. He lies buried in the Palmier graveyard, about two and one-half miles west from the town of Columbia, Monroe county.

JAMES McROBERTS was born in Glasgow, Scotland, in 1760. He came to America and enlisted in the Continental Army when only 18 years of age, serving to the close of the war. He came to Kaskaskia in 1786; in 1797 he resided in Mayesville; was a highly respected citizen. His son, Samuel McRoberts, was elected United States senator from Illinois in 1841. He was pensioned.

MICHAEL MILLER came from Pennsylvania in 1800, settling south of the Moore tract. He served in the Virginia line of troops and was pensioned.

CAPT. JAMES MOORE was born in Maryland in 1750. He came from Kentucky with George Rogers Clark, but returned to his old home. Later he was the leader of a colony, coming to Illinois in 1781 and settled at Bellefontaine, near Waterloo, in Monroe county. He received his commission as captain from Gov. Patrick Henry. He died on the old Moore farm and lies buried in the Bellefontaine cemetery, one miles south of Waterloo.

PETER ROGERS was born in New London, Connecticut, in 1758. He enlisted in 1775, serving until a short time before the close of the war. He was a musician, serving as "Fife Major." He was with Capt. William Coit in a cruise on an armed schooner, when they captured a sloop and a schooner. He was in the battles of Germantown and Monmouth, serving under Capt. Caleb Gibbs in Gen. Washington's Life Guards, with Col. John Drake. He came to Illinois and resided in Waterloo, Monroe county. He was a great patriot and in the campaign of 1840, though an aged man, took an active interest in the campaign, making speeches and in other ways showing his interest. He died very aged, and is buried in Waterloo. He was pensioned.

JOHN WHITESIDE was born in Tryon county, North Carolina. He served from that state and was in the battle of King's Mountain. He removed to Kentucky, where he drew a pension. Coming to Illinois in 1793, he settled in New Design, Monroe county. He afterwards lived at Whiteside's Station and died at Bellefontaine. He is buried in the cemetery one-half mile from the court house, Waterloo.

JOSEPH WRIGHT was a native of Virginia, born in 1760 in Mecklenburg county. He enlisted March, 1780, for three months with Capt. John Thompson, Col. John Glenn; enlisted again in 1781 for three months under Capt. Paul Waddleton, Col. John Glenn. He came to Monroe county to reside and there applied for a pension. The date of his death is not known.

Montgomery County

EZRA BOSTWICK was born in Queen Anne county, Maryland, in 1753. He enlisted under Capt. Patrick Began, North Carolina troops, October 15, 1780, serving under different officers until the close of the war. He came to Illinois, settling in Montgomery county in 1818, in the Bostwick settlement, not far from the present village of Irving. He lies buried in the little graveyard not far from the village of Irving. He was pensioned.

HENRY BRIANCE was a native of North Carolina, where he entered the service in 1777, serving under Col. Wade Hampton, Gen. Thomas Sumpter, and Gen. Francis Marion. He was in the battles of Eutaw Springs, Friday Fort, Thompson's Fort, Monk's Corner and Monroe Field. He came to Montgomery county, Illinois, where he died August 19, 1833, and is buried in the Clear Springs cemetery near where he lived. He was pensioned.

THOMAS BRECKMAN was born in Albermarle county, Virginia. He entered the service early in 1776 under Capt. John Marks, Col. Charles Lewis' regiment, in Gen. Nathaniel Greene's division of the army, serving for three years; he also served under Capt. Archibald Moon, and was in the battles of Brandywine, Germantown, Stony Point and other smaller engagements. He came to Illinois, settling in Montgomery county, where he died, and is buried in a little graveyard which is now a pasture owned by Joseph Spinner. He died about 1838. "Virginia Records."

JOHN CANNADY was born March 14, 1763, in King George's county, Virginia, and entered the service in Bedford county in September, 1781, in Capt. Charles Callaway's company, Col. James Callaway's regiment; was in the siege of Yorktown and served three months. He again enlisted in July, 1782, with Capt. Abraham Kirkpatrick, Col. Christian Fehiger, serving six months. He was transferred to Capt. Charles Yarborough's and Capt. Benjamin Dade's troops and was taken ill and furloughed home. He did garrison duty under Capt. Nathaniel Irish at New London, Campbell county, and was discharged in 1783. He removed to Kentucky, and from there to Montgomery county, Illinois, where he probably died December 15, 1836. He was pensioned.

JOHN CRABTREE was born in Randolph county, North Carolina, May 3, 1763. He entered the service in 1780 under Capt. Edward Williams; he again enlisted under Capt. John Knight. Coming to Illinois, he settled in Montgomery county, in what was known as the "Street Settlement," about four miles from Hillsboro. He was among the early settlers, and lies buried in the family graveyard not far from the old homestead. "North Carolina Records."

THOMAS CRAIG was born in Granville county, North Carolina, October, 1762. He enlisted in 1781, serving in Capt. Smith's company, Col. McKissick's regiment. He re-enlisted in Lincoln county in the Indian spy service, serving under Capt. Brown Stimson and Capt. John Sevier. He came to Illinois, settling in Montgomery county,

East Fork township. The place of his burial is not known. He was pensioned.

BENJAMIN GORDON was born in Newberry county, South Carolina, August 30, 1763. He enlisted in 1780 under Gen. Thomas Sumter, Mecklenburg county, North Carolina. After the battle of Guilford Court House he was sent as wagoner, with the wounded to Gen. Nathaniel Greene's army. Later he served as a mountaineer ranger under Gen. John C. Clark of Georgia. He was discharged in 1783. He came to Montgomery county, Illinois, to reside, living in the Hurricane settlement. He received a pension for his services. The place of his burial is unknown.

WOOTEN HARRIS was a native of Virginia, where he enlisted in Capt. Elliot's company of militia, Brunswick county, in 1777, serving ninety days; he again enlisted under Capt. William Peterson, Col. Charles Harrison's regiment. He served till the close of the war. Coming to Illinois, he settled in Montgomery county in the Hurricane settlement. He died in 1837 and was buried in the Scribner burying ground, Fillmore township, but several years ago his remains were removed to the Fillmore graveyard, where they now repose. He was pensioned.

JOHN LIGET was a native of Virginia, but entered the service under Capt. John Reese in 1776; was transferred to Capt. David Plunkett's company, Fourth Regiment, Light Dragoons of Pennsylvania line of troops. He was taken prisoner in 1778, but soon escaped and rejoined the army under Washington, serving until the close of the war. He was in the battles of White Plains, Trenton, Princeton, Brandywine, Germantown and other smaller engagements. Truly a valiant soldier! He came to Montgomery county, settling in the Bostick settlement. The place of his burial is not known. He was pensioned.

MASON OWENS was born in King's county, Virginia, September 8, 1760. He enlisted three times, serving eight months under Capt. Joseph Rogers, ten months under Capt. George Strother and five months with Capt. William Bunbury, Col. John Skinner. He was in several skirmishes and at the siege of Yorktown. In 1807 he removed to Kentucky, and in 1827 he came to Montgomery county, Illinois, where he died in 1846. He was pensioned.

HARRIS REVIS was born in Northampton county, North Carolina, in 1750. He enlisted under Sergeant Elias Langham, Salisbury, Rowan county, North Carolina, in 1780. He was stationed at the Magazine, where he remained till the close of the war. He came to Illinois with his brother Harry, who is buried in Madison county. Harris Revis settled in Montgomery county, was a commissioner of this county during its early history. He died in 1837 near his home and was buried in the Wright graveyard. "North Carolina in the Revolution."

JAMES RICHARDSON was born in Middlesex county, Virginia, August 25, 1757. He entered the service under Capt. Lemuel Smith, Col. Peter Perkins' regiment, Virginia troops, August, 1780. He also served under Capt. Miner Smith, Gen. Griffith Rutherford's command. He was in the battles of Brick House and Georgetown. Coming to Illinois, he settled in Montgomery county, and died in Hillsboro. He was pensioned.

Moultrie County

JAMES PATTERSON was born in Montgomery county, Virginia, July 5, 1758. He enlisted in 1775 from Rutherford county, North Carolina, serving three months under Capt. James Wilson, Col. John Rutherford's regiment; he again enlisted in August, 1777, for three months under Capt. Jesse Lytle, Col. John Rutherford's regiment; in September, 1780, he again served under Capt. Williams, Col. Arthur Campbell's regiment, serving three months, and finally for the fourth time he served nine months under Capt. Jesse Lytle and Col. Rutherford. He was engaged in the battles of King's Mountain, Cowpens, Guilford Court House and Yorktown. He was wounded at Cowpens and was pensioned. He came to Illinois at an early day, settling in Moultrie county, then a part of Shelby county. He died in 1838 and is buried near Sullivan, Moultrie county. "Virginia Records."

Morgan County

The Rev. James Caldwell Chapter, D. A. R., of Jacksonville observed a red-letter day in their history when on March 10, 1914, a bronze tablet was unveiled in memory of the soldiers of the American Revolution who lie buried in Morgan county.

The exercises were held in the Circuit Court room and were alike impressive and patriotic. The tablet was formally presented by Miss Effie Epler, chairman of the Tablet Committee, and was accepted by the Regent of the Chapter, Mrs. O. F. Buffe, who in turn presented the same to Morgan county.

In behalf of Morgan county, Judge E. P. Brockhouse accepted the tablet. The Hon. Horace Bancroft, a member of the S. A. R., in an address paid an eloquent tribute to the soldiers of '76.

Hon. Richard Yates followed with a stirring address, highly commending the work of Washington, and in an especial manner giving deserved tribute to the women of that period in our history.

Appropriate music was rendered by a concert band and a chorus from the high school. The invocation was given by the Rev. R. O. Post.

The tablet, which was placed on the south wall of the court house, was unveiled by lineal descendants of some of the soldiers commemorated, Miss Anna Clayton and Miss Janette Powell.

ISHMAIL BOBBITT was a native of North Carolina. He was in service under Capt. Farley, and was at the siege of Yorktown. After the war was ended, he removed to Illinois, settling in Morgan county, where he died, and is buried on the Paschal farm near Markham. He was pensioned.

MARTIN BURRIS was born in Pennsylvania in 1754. He served in the Virginia line of troops. He came to Morgan county, Illinois, at an early date and died there in 1839. He was pensioned.

CONSTANTINE CLARKSON was born in Virginia December 18, 1762. He served in the Virginia line of troops. He came to Morgan county, Illinois, to reside, where he died, and lies buried. He was pensioned.

JOHN DAWSON was born in Stafford county, Virginia, July 28, 1750, where he enlisted September, 1775, under Capt. George Williams; he again served from April, 1776, for three months with Capt. George Burrows, and again for one year with Capt. John Mountjoy, and for four weeks under Capt. John James; again from June, 1781, for four months with Capt. George Burrows, and again from the fall of 1781 for four months with Col. Joseph Phillips. A remarkable record of service. He came to Morgan county, Illinois, where he died in 1839, and is buried in the East cemetery, Jacksonville. He was pensioned.

JOSEPH JACKSON was born in Bucks county, Pennsylvania, in 1760. He served in the North Carolina troops. He removed to Sumner county, Tennessee, and from there to Morgan county, Illinois, where he died October 11, 1844. He was pensioned.

SAMUEL JACKSON served in the South Carolina troops in Capt. William Blakeney's company, Harlee's battalion. He came to reside in Morgan county, Illinois, where he died, and is buried in Franklin cemetery, Franklin, Illinois. He was pensioned.

JOB JENKINS was from Virginia, where he served under Col. Daniel Morgan in the Eleventh and Fifteenth Regiments, Company No. 3. He served with Capt. William Johnston and with Capt. Peter Bruin in 1777 and 1778. He removed to West Tennessee, and from there to Morgan county, Illinois, where he died in 1832. He was pensioned.

BOLING JOLLEY was born in Dinwiddie county, Virginia, in 1766, where he enlisted in 1781, and was at the siege of Yorktown. He removed to North Carolina after the war, and from there to Morgan county, Illinois, where he applied for a pension, which was not granted as he had not served six months in the war. He is buried in the Franklin cemetery, and his grave has a government marker. "Pension Reports."

JAMES JORDAN was born near Carlisle, Pennsylvania, November 15, 1755. He served in the South Carolina troops. He came to Morgan county, Illinois, where he died, and is buried on the Massey farm, two miles west of Jacksonville. He was pensioned.

SAMUEL JONES served in the Virginia troops. He came to Morgan county, Illinois, where he died, and is buried on the Paschal farm near Markham. "Virginia Records."

LAWRENCE KILLEBRUE was born May 10, 1763, at Tadbury Town, Edgecomb county, North Carolina. He served in the war from that state. Coming to Illinois, he settled in Morgan county, where he died April 4, 1835. He was pensioned.

DAVID McPETERS enlisted from North Carolina. He was born January 14, 1756, and died in Morgan county, Illinois, March 27, 1846. He was pensioned.

EDMUND MOODY was born in Albermarle county, Virginia, September 18, 1755. He served in the Virginia line of troops. After the war he removed to Kentucky, and from there to Morgan county, Illinois. He died there September 10, 1839. He was pensioned.

PATRICK O'FLYNG was from New Hampshire. He enlisted in Cambridge, Massachusetts, April, 1775, for eight months under Capt. John Moore, Col. John Stark. He served again in 1776 as orderly sergeant with Capt. John Nesmith and Col. Livingston; again in 1777 for six months with Capt. Daniel Livermore, Col. Alexander Scammond; he was also quartermaster sergeant under Capt. Zachariah Beal. He was in service twice from January, 1778, to May, 1778, and from January, 1781, to December, 1781, as sub-conductor of wagons in Gen. Poor's brigade. He was in the battles of Bunker Hill, Quebec, Bemis Heights, and with the Indians on the Susquehanna, under Gen. Sullivan. He removed to Ohio, and from there to Morgan county, Illinois, but died there soon after coming. He died October 7, 1821, aged 71 years. He was pensioned.

THOMAS ROBERTS served in the Virginia troops, and also after the war in the United States Rangers. He removed to Tennessee, and from there to Morgan county, Illinois. "Virginia Records."

JOHN ROBERTSON was born in 1755. He served with the Delaware troops. Coming to Illinois, he resided in Morgan county, where he died, and is buried at Orleans on a farm. He was pensioned.

GEORGE SAUNDERS was in the Virginia Continentals. He also continued in the service after the close of the war. He came to Morgan county, Illinois, and died there in 1820, aged 72 years. "Virginia Records."

WILLIAM SCOTT was born in Virginia in 1755 and served in the war from that state. He came to Morgan county, Illinois, and died there October 4, 1836, and is buried east of Jacksonville, at Orleans, on a farm. He was pensioned.

JARRETT SEYMOUR is said to have been a soldier, but no record of service has been obtained. He is buried five miles south of Franklin in the Providence churchyard. "Family Records."

AUGUSTUS SIMS was born in Virginia May 27, 1763. He enlisted in Henry county in 1781 for three months under Capt. George Hartson and Cols. Abraham Penn and St. George Tucker. He also served three months with Capt. Hayman Crite and Col. Richardson, from July, 1781. He came to Morgan county, Illinois, where he died, and is buried in the Rogers cemetery, south of Waverly. He was pensioned.

ELISHA SMITH served in the New Jersey line of troops. He died in Morgan county, Illinois, and is buried in the Jacksonville cemetery. "New Jersey in the Revolution."

EDMOND STOKES served from Virginia. He came to Morgan county, Illinois, and there applied for a pension. He is buried in Oakland cemetery, Meredosia. "Virginia Records."

ANDREW TURNER was born in North Carolina April 5, 1762, and served from that state during the war. He died in Morgan county, Illinois, August 8, 1842, and is buried in the Rohrer cemetery. He was pensioned.

JOHN WOOD was born in Savannah, Georgia, in 1752. He enlisted twice and was granted 250 acres of land for his war service. He was a member of a scouting party and was entrusted with carrying messages from Gen. Marion to Washington. With his two brothers, William and Nathaniel, he served throughout the war. He also served as paymaster to the First Battalion, Georgia troops, having the rank of captain. He died in Morgan county, Illinois, and is buried in Franklin. "Georgia in the Revolution."

CAPT. JAMES WRIGHT served in the Seventh Virginia Regiment, commanded by Col. John Morgan. He was commissioned second lieutenant July 31, 1776; first lieutenant July 2, 1779. He was a prisoner of war. He died in Morgan county, Illinois, in 1845, and is buried in Franklin. He was pensioned.

Ogle County

DANIEL DAY was born in Keene, New Hampshire, January, 1763. He enlisted April 4, 1780, serving until December under Lieut. Benjamin Ellis and Col. Henry Dearborn. He came to Ogle county, Illinois, and died there in 1838, and was buried in the Daysville cemetery, where a monument has been erected to his memory. "New Hampshire in the Revolution" and "Family Records."

RUFUS PERKINS was a native of Massachusetts, born at Bridgewater about 1763. When very young he enlisted at Ashfield in Capt. Abel Dinsmore's company, serving three months. He again served six months under Capts. Canston and Samuel Hughs. He re-enlisted August 10, 1778, with Capt. Enoch Chapin, serving until January 1, 1779; he again served under Capt. Oliver Shattuck and Lieut. Col. Barnabas Sears, being discharged in 1781. He lived in New York. Coming to Illinois in 1847, he settled at Buffalo Grove, near Polo, Ogle county. This aged veteran made the long journey by stage and steamboat to Chicago, and from there to Buffalo Grove by lumber wagon. He died October 30, 1848. A bronze tablet was placed in the Polo Historical Library in his memory by the Historical Society, assisted by the D. A. R. of Rockford, Rochelle, Freeport and Dixon, and by the Grand Army post. The tablet was unveiled by Edgar Thomas Clinton, a great, great grandson of Rufus Perkins. "Massachusetts in the Revolution" and "County History."

RUFUS PHELPS was born in New York state in 1767, where he enlisted for six months in the Dutchess county troops, and was stationed at Fort Herkimer. He was wounded and was discharged from service, receiving a soldier's bounty. Coming to Illinois, he settled at Holcombe, Ogle county, where he died in 1839. His grave was marked by the Rockford Chapter, D. A. R., June 19, 1909. "New York in the Revolution."

Peoria County

PHINEAS BRONSON was born in Enfield, Connecticut, November 9, 1764, and died in Peoria county, Illinois, October 24, 1845, and is buried in the Princeville cemetery, where a tombstone, upon which is inscribed, "A Soldier of the American Revolution," tells the story of service. He served in the Third Company of the Second Regiment under Major Benjamin Walbridge and Col. Zebulon Butler. He was pensioned.

WILLIAM CROW was born in Rockingham county, Virginia, in 1758, and died in Peoria county, Illinois, January 25, 1854. He is buried in a private cemetery in Limestone township, near Pottstown. He was pensioned.

JOHN DUSENBERRY came from New York, where he served in the war in the Third regiment with Col. Rudolphus Rietzman, enlisting in January, 1776. He was first Lieutenant and then Captain of his company. He was wounded at the battle of White Plains, but again served from December, 1777, to March, 1778. He served under Col. David Van Schaik, Col. Philip Van Courtland, and Gen. Samuel Parsons, for two years under Lafayette. He came to Illinois, residing in Peoria, where he died September 26,

1833, aged 81 years. "New York in the Revolution."

JAMES HARKNESS was a "Minute Man," marching on the first alarm from Pelham, Massachusetts, in Capt. Candless' company, Col. Benjamin Woodbridge's regiment, serving eleven days; he re-enlisted for eight months; and again in June, 1778, serving as corporal and sergeant in Capt. Joseph Perkins' company, Col. Nathaniel Wade's regiment. He was born June 21, 1756, and died at Harkness Grove August 18, 1836, and is buried in the Harkness cemetery, near Trivoli, Peoria county. "Massachusetts Soldiers in the Revolution."

PAULETTE MAILLET was born in 1753 at Mackinac, Michigan. He was an Indian trader and was the founder of Peoria in 1778. Hearing of the defeat of Thomas Brady at St. Joseph, Michigan, in 1777, he decided to revenge the killing of men by the British and Indians. With an armed force they marched to St. Joseph, where they fought like tigers and captured the fort. He returned to Peoria, but lost his life in a quarrel with a Frenchman in 1805. The place of his burial is not known. "County History."

JOHN MONTGOMERY was in the Virginia line of troops. He was born in Virginia in 1764 and died in Peoria county, Illinois, January 26, 1845, and is buried in the Princeville cemetery. "A Soldier of the Revolution" is inscribed on his tombstone. He was pensioned.

ZEALY MOSS was a wagonmaster and assistant quartermaster in the Virginia troops. He enlisted in Loudoun county in the spring of 1777 and served two years. He re-enlisted in 1780 and served to the close of the war. He was born in

Loudoun county, Virginia, March 5, 1755, and died in Peoria county, Illinois, October 30, 1835, and is buried in Springdale cemetery, Peoria. He was pensioned.

Perry County

JOHN BANES was born in Virginia. He enlisted at Mecklenburg in 1779, serving five times for three months each and the sixth time for six months, with Capt. Peter Bennett, and George Ferringot, and Cols. William Moore, Ambrose Ramsey, Joseph Taylor, and Major Joel Lewis. He was in the battle of Camden. He removed to Sumner county, Tennessee, and then to Perry county, Illinois, where he died September 2, 1840. He served in the North Carolina troops. He was pensioned.

LEONARD LIPE was from South Carolina, where he was born about 1755. He served in the troops from that state. After the war he came to Perry county, and settled in Tamaroa township, where he died. He was pensioned.

JOHN MURPHY was born in the North of Ireland. Coming to America, he entered the war and was in the battle of King's Mountain, probably with North Carolina troops. He came to Perry county, Illinois, in 1818, settling near Lost Prairie, where he died. Murphysboro, Jackson county, was named in his honor. "County History."

Pike County

DAVID CALLIS served in the war from Virginia. He again served in the U. S. troops after the close of the War of the Revolution. He came to Pike county, Illinois, to reside, and probably died there. "Virginia Records."

DAVID KEHR was born July 27, 1763, near Philadelphia, Pennsylvania. He enlisted in Northumberland county in April, 1780, serving till August 14, 1780, under Capt. Thomas Gaskin and Col. James Hunter. He was an Indian spy, was taken prisoner and carried to Niagara and kept until July, 1783, when he was set at liberty. Re removed to Ohio, and from there to Pike county, Illinois, where he died after 1839. He is buried near Griggsville. He was pensioned.

JAMES McWITHEY was from New York, where he served in the Charlotte county Militia, in the Seventeenth Regiment, New York troops. He removed to Pike county, Illinois, where he probably died. He was pensioned.

HUGH McNARY was from North Carolina, where he served in the war. He came to Morgan county, Illinois, and there applied for a pension. He died in Pike county, Illinois. He was pensioned.

JOSEPH OLMSTED was from Connecticut, where he served in the Fifth Regiment, commanded by Col. Philip Bradley. He enlisted in Ridgefield. He removed to Pike county, Illinois, and in 1832 applied for a pension, but died before it was granted. "Connecticut in the Revolution."

NATHANIEL PERRIN was from Massachusetts, where he served in the war, enlisting January 6, 1779, serving until June 5, 1780, under Capt. Benjamin Frothingham; he again enlisted, serving from October, 1780, till January, 1781. He removed to Tennessee, where he applied for a pension. He died in Pike county, Illinois. He was pensioned.

ABRAHAM SCHOLL was born December 15, 1765, in Rowan county, North Carolina. He enlisted in 1781 in Fayette county, Virginia, serving several short terms in the Virginia troops under Capts. William Hays, John Constant, Charles Hazelrigg, and John McDowell, with Cols. John Todd, Benjamin Logan, Daniel Boone, and Trotter. He was in the skirmish at Bryant's Station. He came to Pike county and was living at Atlas, where he applied for a pension, but having served less than six months, it was denied. "Pension Reports."

HOWELL SELLERS was born in Charlotte county, North Carolina. He was in the North Carolina troops, was in the battles of Stono, Brier Creek, and the siege of Savannah. He came to Illinois, residing in Pike county, where he died. He was pensioned.

RICHARD TAYLOR was a native of Virginia, where he served as Ensign in the war, enlisting August 4, 1779, in Frederick county. He removed to Illinois, settling in Pike county, where he died very aged. He was pensioned.

Pope County

LUKE DEVOIR was from New Jersey, where he served in the war in Capt. Peter Dickinson's company, Third Battalion, New Jersey troops. He came to Illinois and settled in Pope county, where he died in April, 1827. He was pensioned.

CHARLES DUNN was from Virginia, where he served under Lt. Col. John Cropper. He enlisted November 30, 1778. He continued in the service after the close of the war, and was in the U. S. troops in Pope county, Illinois. "Virginia Records."

BENJAMIN GLOVER served in the war from Virginia, and he also was in the U. S. service after the close of the war. He came to Illinois and resided in Pope county, where he probably died. "Virginia Records."

DANIEL HANCOCK came from Maryland, where he served in the war. Coming to Illinois he located in Pope county, where he probably died, as he was an aged man. He was pensioned.

DAVID McNEELY was from Virginia, where he served in the war. He came to Pope county, Illinois. He was pensioned in 1820 and died the same year in Pope county.

Putnam County

ARCHIBALD ALLEN was born in Virginia in 1749. He served two months in 1781 with Capt. Charles Shelton and Col. Elias Edmonds, in the Virginia troops. He removed to Maryland, then to Kentucky, then to Indiana and later to Putnam county, Illinois, where he applied for a pension. Not having served the required time it was not granted. "Virginia Records" and "Pension Reports."

JOHN EVANS was in the Pennsylvania line of troops. He came to Putnam county and there applied for a pension. "Pennsylvania Archives" and "Pension Reports."

ANDREW MOORE served in the Pennsylvania troops. He came to Putnam county, Illinois, and there applied for a pension. He is buried in Union Grove cemetery. "Pension Reports" and "Pennsylvania Archives."

ISAIAH STRAWN was born in Bucks county, Pennsylvania, October 28, 1758. His parents were Quakers and opposed his enlisting, but when nineteen years of age, he enlisted, serving in the transportation line. At the battle of

Germantown, he rushed into battle, seizing the musket of a fallen comrade and neighbor, who had been mortally wounded. Soon after he was wounded in the left leg, one shot lodging in the hollow of his foot. This he never permitted to be removed, carrying it for sixty-four years. He came to reside in Putnam county, Illinois, where he died August 14, 1843, and is buried in the Florid cemetery, Putnam county. "Pennsylvania Archives" and "Family History."

Randolph County

The history of no part of Illinois exceeds in interest that of the settlement of Randolph county, and Kaskaskia was the great center of interest. Beautiful for situation and as a commercial point, it became alike attractive and prospectively important.

The French here held sway for many years, and were succeeded by the British. Only a few years passed, however, before that intrepid warrior, George Rogers Clark and his band of faithful followers quietly took possession of this part of the territory and planted the Stars and Stripes, in 1778, first at old Fort Massac, then at Kaskaskia. It was but natural that the men who came with Clark should have been charmed with the location and the outlook for future homes for themselves and their families. They were well fitted for the hardships which a new country entailed and for dealing with hostile tribes of Indians which might harrass them. The first considerable American immigration was in 1780 when a colony of pioneer settlers reached Kaskaskia from the Southern states, to be followed by many from the country east of the Alleghanies. Among the number were many soldiers of the American Revolution.

Randolph county is the burial place of many soldiers. Doubtless many were buried where the ever-changing current of the Mississippi river has washed away the land, thus making it impossible to locate their graves. The remains of some of these pioneer-patriots were removed to a cemetery on the hill overlooking the little railroad station called Fort Gage, where the State of Illinois has erected a monument to their memory which bears the following inscription, "Those who sleep here were first buried at Kaskaskia and afterward removed to this cemetery. They planted free institutions in a wilderness and were the founders of a great commonwealth. In memory of their sacrifices, Illinois, grateful, erects this monument. 1892."

In the following lists are many soldiers who came with Clark, and also those who were from the Southern and Eastern states, all of whom lie buried in Randolph county.

JOSEPH ANDERSON was a soldier under George Rogers Clark; he settled on Nine-Mile creek about five miles from Kaskaskia, where he died.

BENJAMIN BYRUM was born in New Castle, Pennsylvania, in 1773. In the spring of 1781 he came to Kaskaskia. He showed his discharge papers from the service and an oath of fidelity taken at Fort Pitt. He did not live long after coming to Illinois.

MELLINGTON COUCH was in the battle resulting in the surrender of Cornwallis. It is not known from what state he enlisted. He is buried at the Preston U. P. cemetery, six miles from

Sparta. He first resided in Marion county. "Family History."

JOHN CLENDENIN was a native of Virginia and served in the troops of that state. After the war he removed to Kentucky, settling in Green county; from there he came to Randolph county, Illinois, locating where the city of Chester now is. He resided on a farm now known as the Porter farm. "Virginia Records."

JAMES CURRY was a soldier with Clark; he settled near the other soldiers with whom he came, not far from Kaskaskia. James Curry had a thrilling experience with the Indians. He and Levi Teel were out hunting and took possession of a cabin built by David Pagan, which was unoccupied, to remain over night. During the night the Indians appeared, and as Teel stood by the door with one foot near the "cat hole," an Indian thrust his spear through his foot; attempting to pull it out, they pinned his hand, thus nailing him to the floor. Curry would not listen to Teel, who advised opening the door, but went to the loft and fired, killing three; he then tumbled the whole roof, as it was not nailed on, down on the Indians, killing the chief and disabling the others which caused the remaining number to flee. Curry helped Teel to reach Kaskaskia, where he remained until he recovered from his wounds. James Curry was chosen by Clark to undertake any desperate or hazardous service. He lived and died on Nine-Mile creek. One day he, with Joseph Anderson, was out hunting. As he never returned, it is supposed that he was killed by the Indians and his body taken away by them. "County History."

JOHN DODGE was a native of Connecticut, was a trader at Sandusky, Ohio, before the Revolutionary War. He strongly favored the cause of the Colonists, and as a result was arrested by the British who carried him to Detroit and later to Quebec, when he escaped in 1779. In that year he was recommended by Washington to Congress as a man who would be useful in the West. He went to Virginia and was appointed Indian agent. Coming to Kaskaskia he rendered aid to Clark in the work there. He died before 1800 and is doubtless buried in Kaskaskia. "County History" and "Connecticut in the Revolution."

JOHN DOYLE was a soldier with Clark. He settled near Kaskaskia. He was a man of some education and taught one of the earliest schools in the county. He was a French scholar. "County History."

ROBERT BRATNEY was born in Ireland. Coming to America he settled in Tennessee where he entered the service. In 1820 he removed to Illinois, settling near the mouth of Little Plum creek in Evansville township. "County History" and "Tennessee Records."

CAPT. JOHN EDGAR was born in Ireland. He was in the British Navy. When the Revolutionary war broke out he was a resident of Detroit. He openly espoused the American cause and was seized by the British commander and sent a prisoner to Quebec; escaping near Montreal he found his way to the American lines. Entering the service he was made Captain in the navy. Coming West in 1784, he settled in Kaskaskia. He was a man of great wealth for those times. During the administration of Governor Arthur St. Clair he was elected to the legislature which convened at Chillicothe, Ohio. After the war he was appointed Major General of the Illinois militia, and in 1790 was made a judge of the "common pleas court." He died in Kaskaskia in 1832. He was pensioned.

JOHN HILTEBRAND and DAVID HIX were soldiers under Clark. Coming to Illinois in 1780, they settled on the east side of Kaskaskia river near the mouth of Nine-Mile creek, where they doubtless died.

WILLIAM FOWLER was born in South Carolina, where he served in the war. He came to Illinois in 1816, locating in the Harmon settlement. In 1825 he was living in the township of Mary, where he doubtless died. He was pensioned. "County History."

PAUL HARROLSON was from South Carolina, where he served in the war. He came to Illinois in 1802, settling on the west side of the Kaskaskia river near the mouth of Camp creek. He was a man of prominence in the early days. In 1809 he acted as Justice of the Peace and from 1803 to 1809 was commissioner and county clerk. He was pensioned. "County History."

DAVID HOAR served from Massachusetts in the Revolutionary war. He remained in the service after the close of the war. Came to Randolph county, Illinois, where he died. "Massachusetts Soldiers and Sailors in Revolutionary War," also "Pension Reports."

JOHN LAWSON served in the Virginia line of troops. He came to Randolph county, Illinois, and there applied for a pension, which was not granted, as he had not served six months. "Virginia Records."

JOHN LIVELY came from South Carolina in 1805; he was in the war from that state. He was seemingly a soldier by nature, as he also served in the war of 1812. He settled in the town of

Central, where he died in 1826. "County History."

CHARLES McNAB was born in Maryland; he enlisted January 7, 1778, was a sergeant in the Sixth Company, First Maryland Regiment, in Capt. Beaty's company; he enlisted again in the Seventh Company of the Third Regiment. He came to Illinois, settling in Randolph county, where he died November 1, 1780. He was pensioned.

HAYDON MILLS, HENRY SMITH and ELIJAH SMITH were soldiers with Clark; returning to Illinois they settled east of Kaskaskia above the mouth of Nine Mile creek. They were doubtless buried there.

JOHN MONTGOMERY was a private with Clark's soldiers, he returned to Illinois, locating four miles from Kaskaskia, where he built a small water mill which was used for many years. He, with many others, was given a tract of land for service in the war. He was a well-known citizen of the county.

DANIEL MURRAY lived in Kaskaskia with his brother William, before the arrival of George Rogers Clark. He gave Clark substantial aid in Kaskaskia; he died there later, being shot in a quarrel over some money affairs. "County History."

DAVID PAGAN was one of Clark's soldiers; coming to Illinois he settled on Nine-Mile creek a few miles from Kaskaskia, where he was doubtless buried.

JAMES and RICHARD PILLARS were from Virginia and served in the war in the Virginia line of troops. In 1781 they were in Fort Massac, Illinois, and in 1793 they removed to Randolph county. James died there in 1833 or 1834. A granddaughter of James remembers that he died while at a celebration, or reunion, of the old soldiers. Their record of service may be found in Virginia in the Illinois papers—D. III.

RAWLEIGH RALLS was born in Virginia, and served in the Virginia troops, enlisting in the latter part of the war, when quite young. After the war he removed to Tennessee, and in 1809 came to Illinois, settling first in Monroe county, but later on the beautiful ridge afterward known as Rall's Ridge. He only lived a few years after coming to Randolph county. "Virginia Records."

ROBERT SEYBOK was with Clark's soldiers; he came to Illinois in 1783, and with other settlers was obliged to take refuge in Kaskaskia on account of the Indians.

WILLIAM SHARP was born in Maryland in 1762. He enlisted in the Fifth Regiment, May 29, 1778. He was made Corporal October, 1781; was discharged May 1, 1781. He removed to Illinois, settling in Randolph county, where he died. He was pensioned.

GEORGE STAMM was born in Maryland, where he enlisted at Frederictown in May, 1780, He was both private and musician with Capt. John Smith and Capt. Christopher Orendorff under Col. John Eccleston in the Sixth Maryland Regiment. He came to Randolph county, settling in Kaskaskia, where he died. He was pensioned.

CAPT. JOHN STEELE was a native of Virginia and served as Captain in the Virginia troops. After the war he removed to Tennessee and in 1789 came to Randolph county, Illinois. He was the founder of Steeleville and died on the farm where he located September 11, 1820. "Virginia Records" and "County History."

JACOB STOPPLEBEAN was born in the state of New York. He enlisted in the Albany county militia, Eighth Regiment, under Col. Robert Van Rensselaer. He again enlisted in the Levies under Col. Marinus Willett. The story is told of him that coming home after his first enlistment he met some of his old home friends who informed him that his wife, supposing him dead, married again and removed to parts unknown. Stopplebean re-enlisted and served to the close of the war. He came to Randolph county, Illinois, where he obtained some land. He died there in 1845, and is buried in what is known as the "Hull Graveyard." He was very eccentric, always sitting with his hat on in the house, claiming to be two years younger than General Washington. "New York in the Revolution" and "Traditional Records."

JOHN STUFFLEBEAN served in the war from Pennsylvania. He came to Randolph county at an early date. He died there January 16, 1844. He was pensioned.

LEVI TEEL was a soldier with Gen. Clark; coming to Illinois he settled on Nine-Mile creek. He was severely wounded by the Indians when James Curry saved his life. He died in Randolph county. "County History."

ALEXANDER WHITTAKER served in the war from Maryland. After the war he came to Randolph county, Illinois, and there applied for a pension. "Pension Reports."

ROBERT WHITEHEAD was a soldier with Clark. He came to Illinois, settling near Kaskaskia, dying there at an advanced age. "County History."

HENRY CRUTCHER and JOHN ROBERTS served with Clark. Roberts was a Lieutenant and Crutcher was Quartermaster, and later was appointed Commissioner. He with Roberts rendered service by purchasing treasury notes to aid in prosecuting the war. Both these men lived in Randolph county long after the close of the war and are doubtless buried near Kaskaskia. "County History."

The records of the French who were loyal to the American cause are mostly lost.

Col. Clark, soon after taking Kaskaskia, appointed several men as officers to recruit companies to aid in the conquest of Vincennes. Among the number was Francis Charleville, who was appointed Captain. He raised 50 men who enlisted for eight months from January, 1779. Of the little band of 50 men, only 28 returned to Illinois, and of this number 10 resided in Kaskasia after the war, and were listed as heads of families or members of the Militia later. It would be manifestly unjust to make no mention of these loyal French subjects of the American cause, and we must conclude that the men whose names are here presented were buried in Randolph county, in or near Kaskaskia.

    Bazelle Allere
    Michael Antere
    Daniel Blouin
    Antoine Bienvenue, Sr.
    Jerome Danis
    Joseph Danis or Daney
    Michael Danis
    Antoine Lavigne

Joseph Richard
Joseph Toulouse

JOSEPH ALLERE was a soldier under Clark and lived in Kaskaskia long after the war.

JEAN BAPTISTE BARBAU, Sr., was from New Orleans, born in 1722. He was Commandant at Prairie du Rocher, a justice and deputy county lieutenant. His will is recorded in Randolph county. He died in 1810.

JEAN BAPTISTE CHARLEVILLE and MICHAEL GODIN were officers appointed by Colonel Todd. They lived in Kaskaskia after the close of the war and were heads of families.

NICHOLAS JANIS was made Captain and resided in Kaskaskia after the close of the war. It is not known where he died.

Saline County

REUBEN BROMLET served in the war from Virginia. He came to what was then Gallatin county, but now is in Saline county, settled in Raleigh township, coming in 1819. He died there and is buried in the Bromlet graveyard. He was a very aged man. He was pensioned.

THOMAS HAMILTON was born in New Jersey December 24, 1762. He served in the war from North Carolina, enlisting August, 1780, and served three months with Capt. Arthur Forbus under Col. John Paisley. He again served three months under Col. William R. Davie, in Capt. James Wilson's company. He again served from December 1, 1780, for five months in Capt. David Gillaspie's company, and Col. Paisley's regiment. He once more served from March, 1782, for two months under Cols. Edward Gwin and William Washington, also for a few days with Lieut. George Parkes. He came to what is now Saline county, where he died February 14, 1841. He was pensioned.

LEWIS HOWELL served from Virginia. He removed to Kentucky and from there came to what is now Saline county, where he probably died. He was pensioned.

WILLIAM ROARK was born in New Jersey, June, 1760. He served in the war four different times eight months until 1782. He was under Capt. John Fleet, Mark Thompson, John Maxfield, and Michael Catt. He served under Gen. George Rogers Clark, was taken prisoner, carried to Detroit and Canada, was paroled in 1783. He came to Gallatin county, Illinois, but died in Saline county, March 4, 1841. He was pensioned.

Sangamon County

On October 19, 1911, the 130th anniversary of the surrender of Lord Cornwallis, the Sons and Daughters of the American Revolution of Springfield, dedicated a bronze tablet upon which were the names of the soldiers of the War for Independence who are buried in Sangamon county. The tablet was placed upon the base of one of the stone columns at the south entrance of the court house. The exercises were held in the circuit court room which has become memorable in the history of Sangamon county. Col. Charles F. Mills, president of the S. A. R. of Springfield, presided at the meeting and introduced the speakers.

PROGRAM

Invocation—Rev. George C. Dunlop.
Song (Quartet)—America.
Introductory Remarks—Col. Charles F. Mills, President Sons of the American Revolution.
Greetings from the State of Illinois—Hon. Charles S. Deneen, Governor of Illinois.
Greetings from Illinois Daughters of the American Revolution—Mrs. George A. Lawrence, State Regent.
Song—Quartet.
Historical Sketch of the Revolutionary Soldiers buried in Sangamon County—Mrs. Edwin S. Walker.
Song—"Freedom's Sons," words by Mrs. George Clinton Smith. Tune, "Illinois."
Dedicatory Address—Hon. William A. Northcott.
Poem—Mrs. George Clinton Smith.
Presentation of the Tablet to Sangamon County—Mrs. James H. Paddock, Regent, Springfield Chapter Daughters of the American Revolution.
Unveiling of the Tablet, by Mary Lawrence Radcliff, and Harold C. George, descendants of Joel Maxcy, and Philip Crowder.
Acceptance of the Tablet on behalf of Sangamon County—B. L. Barber, Esq., Chairman of Board of Supervisors.

ISAAC BAKER was born in Fredericktown, Maryland. He served as a fifer during the last two years of the war. It is not known in what regiment he served. The Maryland records are far from complete. He came to Illinois in 1828, settling in Rochester township where he died in 1848, aged 96 years. So thoroughly was he imbued with the spirit of patriotism, that in the Harrison campaign of 1840, at the advanced age of 88 years, yet with the ardor of a lad, he rode through the streets of Springfield in a log cabin drawn by thirty-two yoke of oxen; the cabin was lined with deer and coon skins, while the barrel of cider with which the campaigners were regaled, spoke eloquently of the apple crop in the forties. Isaac Baker is buried in the Rochester cemetery. "County and Family Histories."

MOSES BROADWELL was a native of New Jersey, born in Elizabethtown, in 1764. He entered the army when a mere lad, serving a limited time near the close of the war in the Third New Jersey Regiment under Col. Elias Dayton, 1780. He came to Illinois in 1820, settling near Pleasant Plains, where he died in 1827. He is buried in Oak Ridge cemetery, Springfield. "New Jersey in the Revolution."

GEORGE BRYAN—A native of North Carolina, born in 1758. When quite young, he removed with his parents to Virginia and from there to Kentucky in 1781. He rendered service in defending the Fort, which was named in his honor, against an attack by the Indians. The bravery of one of the young maidens exhibited during this attack of the Indians, won the heart of young Bryan, and a wedding followed in the early autumn. In 1834, Mr. Bryan came to Sangamon county with his children and grand children, dying in 1845, and is buried in the Woodside burying ground. He was pensioned.

JOHN BURTON — Born in Mecklinburg county, Virginia, in 1761, enlisted from that county in 1780, for three months in Capt. Asa

Oliver's company, Col. Charles Fleming's regiment, and again in 1781, for three months in Stephen A. Berry's company, Virginia troops. He was at the siege of Yorktown. A pension was granted him in 1833, then a resident of Sangamon county. He died here in 1839; is buried in Chatham township. He was pensioned.

ENOS CAMPBELL — A Scotchman, early espoused the cause of the Colonies, enlisting in New Jersey, serving six years, for which service he was pensioned. After the war he removed to Pennsylvania and from there to Ohio, thence to Sangamon county in 1835, settling in Gardner township. Mr. Campbell lies buried in Salisbury township. He was pensioned.

CHRISTIAN CARVER—A native of Northampton county, Pennsylvania, born in 1759, entered the service in Surrey county, North Carolina, serving three months from August, 1777, in Capt. Henry Smith's company, and again for the same length of time, November, 1777, in Capt. John Crouse's company. Mr. Carver removed to Sangamon county, where he died and is buried in Clear Lake township. His widow, a second wife, received a pension at his death.

BAZEL, or BARZILLA CLARK, was born in Pennsylvania in 1750; he was married in 1773 to Nancy — — —, who endured peculiar hardships during the war, being confined in a fort where for two weeks she subsisted on parched corn and water. Bazel Clark acted as private in Pennsylvania Militia, Washington county, Pennsylvania. They came to Sangamon county in 1821, settling in Salisbury township, where he died September 24, 1840. "Pennsylvania Archives."

MICHAEL CLIFFORD—Born in New Jersey in 1759, enlisted in North Carolina in 1775, serving to the close of the war, was attached to Capt. John Johnson's company in Col. Francis Locke's regiment, was in the battle of Pedee river, and the expedition against the Cherokees in Tennessee. After his death in Sangamon county, Illinois, in 1835, his widow was allowed his pension.

PHILIP CROWDER—Born near Petersburg, Virginia, in 1759, was a true patriot. An elder brother was drafted for the service, but as he had a family, Philip volunteered to serve in his place. Mr. Crowder was present at the surrender of Cornwallis. He was pensioned while living in Sangamon county in 1833, he died in 1844, and is buried in a family burying ground west of the city of Springfield.

AQUILLA DAVIS was born in St. Mary's county, Maryland. He was early taken by his parents to Farquier county, Virginia. He enlisted March 19, 1781, under Lieuts. Robert Craddock, and Luke Cannon, with Col. Thomas Posey, in the Virginia line of troops. Aquilla Davis came to Illinois in 1820, settling near Elkhart; he removed to Fancy Creek township, then back to Elkhart, where he died August 15, 1831. From the family records. it appears that he was buried in Wolf Creek cemetery in Sangamon county. He was pensioned.

JAMES DINGMAN—Born in Northampton county, Pennsylvania, in 1758, entered the service there in 1778, in Captain John Van Etten's fourth compay, Col. Jacob Stroud's regiment, sixth battalion. Near Riverton in Sangamon county, in a family burying ground, rises a marble shaft which marks his last resting place, bearing the following inscription: "James Dingman died September 3rd, 1836, aged 79 years, 11 months and 3 days; a Revolutionary patriot who fought the battles of this country without reward save a consciousness of duty well done." "Pennsylvania in the Revolution."

ROBERT FISK was one among those who heard the tocsin of the American Revolution sounded April 19, 1775, at Lexington, Mass., his place of residence. Serving as a "minute man," he later enlisted for the entire war, was a sergeant in Capt. Joshua Walker's company, David Green's regiment. He was pensioned while a resident of Sangamon county, Illinois. The date of his death is not known.

JAMES HAGGARD was born in Albermarle county, Virginia, in 1757. He enlisted from that county in 1780, and again in 1781 in Col. John Lindsey's regiment. Capt. John Henderson's company. He came to Sangamon county, Illinois, to reside and died in Gardner township in 1843, and is buried in that township. A stone marks his grave. He was pensioned.

WILLIAM HAILE served in the war from Virginia, Richmond county. He was also retained in the service after the close of the war, and was killed by the Indians in 1832. He came to Sangamon county, Illinois, and is probably buried there. "Virginia and Pension Records."

EZEKIEL HARRISON was a soldier in the Virginia line of troops; he was wounded in the battle of Point Pleasant. Coming to Illinois with his wife, three sons and one daughter, in 1822, he settled in Cartwright township, where he died in 1836, and is buried on the farm where he settled. His father, Thomas Harrison, was the founder of Harrisonburg, Virginia. "Virginia Records."

THOMAS JAMES served in the war from Pennsylvania. He came to Sangamon county, Illinois, and died in Rochester November 2, 1833. He was pensioned. "Pennsylvania Archives."

WILLIAM JONES was born in Dansbury, Bucks county, Pennsylvania, March 13, 1744, but enlisted in the New Jersey line of troops in 1774 for one year with Capt. John B. Scott. He again enlisted in 1775 with Capt. John Seward, and Col. Ephraim Martin for five months, and he also served as waiting man for Gen. Putnam. He was in the battle of White Plains. He came to Sangamon county, Illinois. "Pension Reports."

JOHN LOCKRIDGE was born in Augusta county, Virginia. He early enlisted in the service, and was in many battles, principally Guilford Court House, and the Cowpens. In 1835 he came to Sangamon county, Illinois, with four sons and four daughters, settling in Ball township, where he died in 1848, aged 87 years. He was pensioned.

ABRAM LUCAS was born in 1756 in Pennsylvania. He enlisted in Capt. Brinton's company, Col. Lachlen McIntosh's regiment, serving four months on the frontier of Pennsylvania and also during an expedition against the Indians. He served as an Indian spy. He removed to Sangamon county, Illinois, and in 1836 he applied for a pension which was not granted, as he had served less than six months. "Pension Reports."

THOMAS MASSIE was born in Albermarle county, Virginia, where he entered the service.

At the close of the war he removed to Kentucky, and from there to Sangamon county, Illinois, settling in Curran township, where he died in 1835, and is buried in the Salem burying ground in Curran. He was pensioned.

JOEL MAXCY was born in Rockingham county, Virginia, in 1761. He enlisted in the Virginia line of troops, and was in the battle of Guilford Court House. He removed to Kentucky, and from there to Sangamon county, Illinois, where he died in 1844, aged 83 years. His memory of distinguished officers was clear. He is buried in the old Salem burying ground, where a government marker is placed at his grave. He was pensioned.

PETER MILLINGTON was a native of faraway Vermont, and was in the service from that state, accompanying Ethan Allen and Benedict Arnold on their expedition to Quebec, was taken prisoner, but when he was released he again entered the service, enlisting under Capt. William Hutchin's company. He was made sergeant, and later lieutenant. He came to Ohio, and from there to Sangamon county, Illinois, settling in Cotton Hill township. He only lived a short time, and is buried in the township where he settled with his son. "Vermont in the Revolution" and "Family History."

JOHN PEAKE was born in 1756 in Fairfax county, Virginia. He enlisted for six months under Capt. Henry Lee. Owing to ill health he was discharged, but having recovered his health, he again enlisted in September, 1777, for three months under Capt. Benjamin Harrison, Major Martin Pickett. He removed to Kentucky and was there granted a pension in 1833. He removed to Sangamon county, Illinois, in 1730, settling in Salisbury, where he died December 21, 1841, and was buried in the old Salisbury burying ground, where his grave can still be seen. He was pensioned. John Peake kept a diary for many years which is of great interest. He never married.

WILLIAM PENNY was born in North Carolina in 1751. He served as captain of a cavalry company, and passed through great privations during the war. He removed to Pope county, Illinois, and from there to Sangamon county, settling on Richland Creek, where he died, and is buried in the Richland cemetery, Cartwright township. A stone marks his grave. He was pensioned.

GEORGE PULLIAM came from Virginia, where he served in the war. He was granted a tract of land for his services. He came to Sangamon county, Illinois, and is doubtless buried there. "Virginia Records."

JOHN PURVINES was a native of Lancaster county, Pennsylvania, born in 1763, enlisted in North Carolina, serving three years under Cols. William Davis and Wade Hampton, with Capts. James White, William Penny, and Robert Burns. He was in the battle of Camden and in the last skirmish of the revolution, at Stono Ferry, South Carolina. He was given a pension after residing in Sangamon county, he died in 1833, and is buried in the Richland cemetery, Cartwright township.

WILLIAM RALSTON was a native of Virginia, enlisted there when young, was present at the surrender of Cornwallis; he removed to Kentucky, and in 1828, came to Gardner township, Sangamon county, Illinois. He died in 1835, and is buried in the Morgan cemetery, Gardner township. He was pensioned.

THOMAS ROYAL was born in Manchester, England, 1758. Coming to America, he, with a comrade, enlisted in the war for Independence. The friend was instantly killed in battle and Mr. Royal was wounded in the ankle. At the close of the war, he removed from Virginia to Ohio, and from there to Ball township, Sangamon county, Illinois, where he died in 1834, is buried in the Brunk cemetery, Ball township. He was pensioned.

JOHN STRINGFIELD was born in North Carolina about 1760. He served in the North Carolina troops, and was in the battle of King's Mountain, October 7, 1780. He came to reside in Sangamon county in December, 1821, but only lived nine days, dying January 5, 1822. He lies buried nine miles northeast of Springfield. "Family History."

JOHN WHITE was in the Pennsylvania line of troops in Capt. Benjamin Loxley's company. He enlisted in 1776, was pensioned while a resident of Sangamon county, Illinois, died here October, 1853, aged 92 years.

WILLIAM CASSADY and JAMES WADDELL are said to have served in the war, and both are buried in Rochester. "Traditional Records."

There were present at the unveiling ceremony, descendants of more than half the soldiers whose names are engraved upon the tablet; aged men and women came from long distances to attend the exercises given in honor of their Revolutionary ancestors.

Schuyler County

DAVID BLAIR was said to have been a soldier from Pennsylvania but no record of service has been obtained. He died in Schuyler county. "County History."

WILLIAM BLAIR was born in Lancaster county, Pennsylvania, in 1760. He enlisted from Cumberland county, May, 1778, serving as a substitute for his father, Alexander, serving two months. In May, 1779, he again enlisted under Gen. John Sullivan, he again served seven months on the frontier until 1781. He came to Schuyler county, Illinois, where he died. He was pensioned.

A. W. CAVALEY was from Virginia, where he served as agent for James Stewart's Artillery of Virginia. He came to Schuyler county, Illinois, where he died. He was pensioned.

BENJAMIN CARPENTER was from Virginia, where he enlisted May, 1776. He served when Cornwallis surrendered. He came to Schuyler county, Illinois, where he died. He was pensioned.

HENRY GREENE was from Maryland where he enlisted in 1779 under Col. Thomas Wolford in the Second Regiment Maryland troops. He was discharged at Annapolis. He came to Schuyler county, Illinois, where he died May 1, 1837. He was pensioned.

JAMES LANMAN enlisted at Charlestown, South Carolina, July, 1776. He was an orderly sergeant in the First Regiment of South Carolina troops. He again enlisted in March, 1781, in North Carolina, under Col. Nathaniel Greene, was in the battles of Guilford Court House, and

Eutaw Springs, where he was wounded in the thigh. He came to Schuyler county, Illinois, where he died. He was pensioned.

GEORGE TAYLOR served in the war from Virginia, enlisting in 1777, under Col. Daniel Broadhead, and Gen. Lachlan McIntosh. He also served in Pennsylvania in 1778, and helped to guard the prisoners at Saratoga. He came to Schuyler county, Illinois, where he died. He was pensioned.

Scott County

NICHOLAS CURRY served in the war from South Carolina. He removed to Lincoln county, Tennessee, but came to Illinois in 1832, settling in Coles county, and from there to Scott county, where he died September 16, 1848. He is buried in the McAlebs graveyard, one and one-half miles north of the town of Bluffs. A stone marks his grave. "Family and County Histories."

JAMES McEVERS was born in Massachusetts, where he enlisted from the town of Hancock to serve three years in Capt. William Lusk's company, and Col. Benjamin Simond's regiment. He removed to Ohio, and from there to Morgan county, Illinois, but died in 1829 in Scott county. He was pensioned.

SOLOMON PATTERSON served in the war from Pennsylvania in First Company, Fourth Battalion, Cumberland county, under Capt. John McConnell, and Col. Samuel Culbertson. He came to Monroe county, Illinois, but removed to Scott county, where he died at the residence of his daughter, Mrs. McCracken, in the town of Manchester. "Pennsylvania Archives."

JESSE STOUT served in the war from New Jersey. He came to Illinois, settling in Morgan county. He is probably buried in Scott county, as his widow drew a pension there. He was pensioned.

JOSEPH SUMMERS was born in Kent county, Delaware in 1749, but enlisted in North Carolina, in Guilford county, serving three months under Capt. Thomas Flack, and Col. James Martin. He again enlisted for six months under Capt. Edward Gwynn, and again for three months with Capt. Elliott, and Col. Henry Lee. He came to Morgan county, Illinois, but died in Scott county, and is buried there. He was pensioned.

Shelby County

ELIJAH BIGGS served in the war from North Carolina. He came to Shelby county, Illinois, and there applied for a pension, but having served less than six months, it was not granted. "North Carolina and Pension Records."

JOHN JENKINS was from Hardy county, Virginia, where he served in the war. He came to Shelby county, Illinois, and died there very aged. He was pensioned.

OBADIAH WADE served in the Virginia Militia. He removed to Kentucky and there was given a pension. He came to Shelby county, Illinois, and doubtless died there. He was pensioned.

St. Clair County

When Illinois was admitted to the Union in 1818, nine-tenths of the population was south of the geographical center, and the entire State north of where Shelbyville now is, was almost a wilderness, there being few settlements.

To Randolph and St. Clair counties belong the honor of the earliest settlements, and in these two counties are a larger number of Revolutionary soldiers buried than in any counties of the State.

ELEAZER ALLEN was a native of Connecticut, born in 1755. He enlisted May 1, 1775, for eight months with Capt. James Chapman; again Jan. 1, 1776, for one year under the same captain, and with Col. Samuel Parsons in what was known as "Parson's Continentals." He was in the battles of New York, King's Bridge, and White Plains.

He early came to Illinois, settling in St. Clair county, where he applied for a pension. He died in 1828 and is buried in Shiloh Precinct.

NATHANIEL BELL was born March 5, 1755, in Warren county, North Carolina. He enlisted in Anson county, April 1, 1776, serving fourteen months under Capt. Thomas Potts, Col. Isaac Huger, South Carolina troops; he enlisted again September, 1781, for two months with Capt. Thomas Harris, Col. William Loften, North Carolina troops. He came to Illinois, settling in St. Clair county, where he died January 17, 1835. He was pensioned.

THOMAS BRADY was a resident of Cahokia before the Revolution. Learning of the struggle of the colonies, he raised a small company of men in 1777 and marched to St. Joseph, Michigan. They captured the garrison, but returning, they were overtaken at Calumet and in a skirmish which ensued, two were killed and Brady was taken prisoner. The following year he escaped and finally reached Cahokia. He served under Col. Clark and was elected sheriff of St. Clair county. He died in Cahokia. "State and County Histories."

M. BOISMENUE was one of the soldiers with Thomas Brady in the expedition against St. Joseph, Michigan. He was wounded and remained with the Indians all winter, returning to Cahokia in the spring. He also served with Col. Clark. He died in Cahokia.

MRS. THOMAS BRADY was better known as Madam La Compt. She was born of French parents in 1734, at St. Joseph, Michigan. She removed to Cahokia, Illinois, in 1770. She rendered distinct service to the Americans by preventing Indian outbreaks during the Revolutionary War. After the death of Mr. Brady she took the name of her second husband, La Compt. She died in 1843 in Cahokia, aged 109 years. "County History."

JOSEPH CARR was born in Virginia in 1752, served in the Virginia troops. After the war he came to Illinois in 1793, settling in Freeburg, St. Clair county, where he died March 6, 1817. "Virginia Records."

JOHN COLLINSWORTH was born in Virginia in 1761 and served with the Virginia troops. After the war he removed to Claiborne county, Tennessee, and from there came to St. Clair county, Illinois, where he died. He was pensioned.

JOHN CONN was a soldier with Colonel Clark. He settled in Cahokia and died there in 1780.

NICHOLAS HORNER was born in England. He came to America and enlisted in the Pennsylvania line of troops, serving as a ranger on the frontier. He also served in the 4th Pennsylvania Battalion from Jan. 3, 1776, to Jan. 3, 1777, with Col. Anthony Wayne. He was living in Maryland in 1790, but removed to Lebanon, St. Clair county, Illinois, about 1814. He died aged 85 years, and is buried near Lebanon. "Pennsylvania Archives."

JOSEPH JONES was a native of Maryland. He enlisted May 30, 1778, for three years in Pulaski's Loyal Legion. He served as a substitute from Anne Arundel county, Maryland. He came to St. Clair county, Illinois, to reside and died there August 26, 1826. He was pensioned in St. Clair county in 1823.

THOMAS KNIGHTEN was a native of South Carolina; was sergeant in the Continental troops. He came to St. Clair county, Illinois, and died there. He was born in 1750; was pensioned.

JOSEPH LAMBERT was from Virginia and served from that State. He came to St. Clair county, Illinois, to reside, where he died. "History of St. Clair County" and "Virginia Records."

RISDON MOORE. The Moore family came to America from Wales in 1732, settling in Delaware. Risdon Moore was born in Delaware, Nov. 20, 1760. He entered the United States Navy at the age of 16 years and served during the war. He removed to North Carolina, then to Georgia, and later to St. Clair county, Illinois. He was speaker of the Illinois House of Representatives in 1814, and was a member of the first, third and fourth Legislatures. He was strongly opposed to making Illinois a slave state. He was the great grandfather of Gov. Charles S. Deneen. He died in 1828 and is buried three miles east of Bellville.

REV. EDWARD MITCHELL was born in Cecil county, Maryland, August 3, 1760; removed with his parents to Virginia, settling in Fincastle, Botetourt county. He enlisted first as a private, then corporal, and was made captain of the First Virginia Rifles; was in the battles of Guilford Court House and Haw River. He was also quartermaster in Col. William Campbell's regiment. He came to St. Clair county, Illinois, in 1818, settling at Turkey Hill. He died December 3, 1837, and is buried on a farm near Belleville. "Virginia Records."

LIEUTENANT JAMES MITCHELL was born in Cecil county, Maryland, March, 1727. He was the father of Edward, and came with him to St. Clair county, Illinois, in 1818. He served in the Albemarle Barracks, was also in the battles of Guilford Court House and Clover Lick, May 1, 1780. Is buried near Belleville. "Virginia Records" and "Family History."

CAPTAIN JOSEPH OGLE was born in Virginia. He commanded a company of Virginia troops. His commission was signed by Patrick Henry and is now in the possession of a descendant. He came to Illinois in 1785 from Wheeling, Virginia, settling first in New Design. In 1802 he was a pioneer in locating in Ridge Prairie, near the present town of O'Fallon, where he died in 1821. Captain Ogle was one of the prominent citizens of St. Clair county. "Virginia Records."

WILLIAM PADFIELD was born in Maryland. He enlisted in the Revolutionary War and served as a driver of a provision wagon. He removed to Kentucky, and from there came in 1815 to Illinois, settling in Summerfield, where he died, aged 75 years, and is buried three miles south of Summerfield. "County History."

DAVID PHILLIPS was born in Orange county, North Carolina, in 1755. He served in the North Carolina troops, but after the war removed to Kentucky, and then to St. Clair county, Illinois, settling on Richland Creek, north of Belleville. He died in 1826 on the farm where he settled. "County History."

CAPTAIN JAMES PIGGOTT was born in Connecticut. He served in the privateering business; removed to Westmoreland county, Pennsylvania, where he commanded a company, being made captain April 6, 1776, serving under General St. Clair. He was in the battles of the Brandywine, Saratoga and other skirmishes. He followed General St. Clair to the west and was placed in command of Fort Jefferson, five miles below the mouth of the Ohio River. He came to St. Clair county and established a fort in 1783, west of Columbia, Monroe county. In 1795 he built a ferry between East St. Louis and St. Louis. He died in East St. Louis in 1799. "Connecticut in the Revolution" and "County History."

JOHN PRIME (OR PRIMM) was born in Stafford county, Virginia. He served in the Virginia troops and was pensioned for service. He came to St. Clair county, Illinois, in 1803, settling near Belleville, where he died in 1836, aged 87 years. He was present at the surrender of Cornwallis. He was pensioned.

JOHN PULLIAM was born in Botetourt county, Virginia. He served in the Virginia troops in the war; removed to Kentucky and from there came to New Design, Monroe county, in 1796. Later he lived in Fayetteville, St. Clair county, where he died in 1813. "Virginia Records," "Family History."

MARTIN RANDLEMAN was native of South Carolina, and served from that state in the Revolutionary War. He came to Illinois in 1801 and a year later settled in Belleville. He drew a pension in 1831, and died in St. Clair county.

SAMUEL REDMON served in the war from Virginia; he came from Rockingham county to St. Clair county, Illinois, where he applied for a pension, but it was not granted as he had not served six months. "Virginia Records" and "Pension Rolls."

HOSEA RIGGS was born in Virginia in 1760. He served in the Pennsylvania line of troops. He came to Illinois in 1796, settling in the American Bottom, Monroe County; later he removed to St. Clair county and lived two miles east of Belleville, where he died October 29, 1841, very aged. He was an exhorter in the Methodist Church and was the first minister of that denomination in the county. He was pensioned.

LARKIN RUTHERFORD was one of George Roger Clark's soldiers; was at the storming of Fort Sackville in 1779. He came to St. Clair county in 1800, settling north of Belleville, where he resided for many years, and where he died.

COL. JOHN THOMAS, JR., was in the South Carolina troops. He served with his father, Col. John Thomas, and when his father was taken prisoner in 1780, he succeeded him in the command of the regiment. He is known as the "Hero of Cedar Springs." He came to reside in St. Clair county, Illinois, and was made treasurer of the Territory, and later of the State. He died in Shiloh and is buried in the church yard. He died in 1919. "Carrington's Battles of the Revolutionary War."

BENJAMIN WEST was born in Maryland in 1743. He removed to Botetourt county, Virginia, and entered the service there. He was on the staff of Gen. George Washington. He came to Illinois in 1818, settling in St. Clair county, near Belleville. He died there, a very aged man. "Virginia Records."

The French in St. Clair County

Many French inhabitants of St. Clair county rendered service to Col. George Rogers Clark. Some remained in the county after the close of the war, while many removed to other states and died there. It is reasonable to suppose that the following lived and died in St. Clair county:

MICHEL BEAULIEU was a justice in Clark's court and later was elected justice in the court of the district in 1779. He died in Cahokia soon after this date.

ANTONIE and JOSEPH CESIRE, father and son, were from Lachine, Canada. Both aided Colonel Clark. Antoine was the most important citizen in Cahokia in 1778. He died in 1779. Joseph was one of the justices in 1781.

JEAN BTE. DUBUQUE was a native of Montreal. He was several times elected justice and greatly aided Clark. After the close of the war he was made commandant.

ANTOINE GIRADIN was a prominent citizen of the community. He was a justice in Clark's court, and was elected a justice of the court of the District of Cahokia in 1779, serving several times in this office. He died in 1802.

TURANJEAU GODIN gave financial aid to the Americans and was a justice in Clark's court; also appointed captain at Cahokia. His heirs were living in 1783 in Cahokia.

JEAN BTE. LA CROIX gave financial aid to the Americans, and was a justice in Clark's court.

JOSEPH PELTIER was a soldier under Colonel Clark. He remained in Illinois and was living in St. Clair county after the close of the war; was a member of the militia in 1790.

FRANCIS TROTTIER was one who gave financial aid to the Americans, and was made commandant of Cahokia. He died in Cahokia previous to 1783.

JEAN BTE. SAUCIER was a military engineer. He came to Illinois at an early day and planned Fort de Chartres in 1752. He removed to Cahokia. His son, named for him, was one of the first judges in Cahokia. He died in Cahokia.

Tazewell County

ELLIOT GRAY was born in Pelham, Massachusetts, Sept. 17, 1755, where he enlisted under Capt. Elijah Dwight, in the Massachusetts troops. He came to Illinois, settling in Tazewell county, where he died and is buried near Armington. The Peoria chapter D. A. R. have marked his grave. He was pensioned.

SAMUEL McCLINTOCK was from Virginia, where he was born in Augusta county, in 1763. He served three different times in 1781 under Capts. James Trimble, William Smith, and

William Kincaid, with Cols. Sampson Matthews, William Boyer, and Samuel Vance. He was in the siege of Yorktown. He removed to Tazewell county, Illinois, where he died. He was living in 1840. "Pension Reports."

DAVID SHIPMAN was from Virginia where he served in 1780 in Capt. Robert Craven's Rifle company. He served on an alarm towards Blue Ridge, and also with his wagon hauling for the army. He removed to Fayette county, Illinois, and from there to Tazewell county, where he died, and is buried in the Antioc cemetery. He was pensioned.

Union County

ALEXANDER BEGGS was born in Antrim county, Ireland, May 30, 1754. Coming to America he entered the service of the colonies and served in 1776 for four months in Henry Lee's Artillery company; he again enlisted in 1778 for three months and in 1781 for the same period, he also served ten months in 1777. He was captured at Brandywine but escaped that night. He was also in the battle of Stono. He served first in the Pennsylvania troops. After the war he removed to Union county, Illinois, where he died Feb. 4, 1837. He was pensioned.

JOSEPH EDWARDS was from Virginia, where he enlisted for nine months in 1776 under Col. Adam Slencar, was discharged at Martinsburg, Virginia. He came to Union county Illinois, in 1829. When he applied for a pension he stated that his property consisted of one bed worth $3.00; one axe worth $2.00; one plow worth $3.00 and one hoe valued at $1.00, making a sum total of $9.00. He died in Union county. He was pensioned.

JOHN ELLIS was born March 9, 1735, in Frederick county, Virginia. He enlisted in Greenbrier county, serving as an Indian spy from 1773 to 1783; was appointed by Gen. Andrew Lewis and served at Ellis' Fort under Capt. John Cook. He came to Illinois and resided in Union county, where he died May 29, 1834. He was pensioned.

JACOB FRICK was a native of Pennsylvania, where he was born about 1747; he enlisted in the Lower Milford township company, Buck's county, in 1775, under Capt. Harry Huber; he also served under Gen. Griffith Rutherford. In 1823 he came to Illinois settling in Jonesboro precinct, where he died. He was pensioned.

JOHN HARGRAVE was born Nov. 23, 1755, in South Carolina, near the line of North Carolina. He enlisted in 1776 for two and one half months with Capt. Dennis Haukins, and Col. Daniel Horry; again in 1780 for ten months with Capt. Thomas Hemphill and Col. Francis Locke; again in 1781 for six months with Capt. Francis Boykin and Col. Charles Middleton. He was in the battles of Ramsour's Mill and Eutaw Springs. He came to Union county, Illinois, in 1809, and is probably buried there. He was pensioned.

ELIAS HOUSE was from North Carolina, where he served in the war. He lost an arm in the service. Coming to Illinois, he settled in Union county, where he died very aged. He was pensioned.

CHRISTOPHER LYERLE was born in 1764 in North Carolina, where he enlisted in 1780 when only 16 years of age in the North Carolina troops in Capt. Archibald Lytle's company and Col. John G. McRae's regiment, serving eighteen months. He came with many others to Union county, where he died. He was pensioned.

PETER MEISENHEIMER came from Cabarras county, North Carolina, where he enlisted in the North Carolina troops. He removed to Union county, Illinois, in 1819 settling in what became known as the Meisenheimer precinct, where he died. He was pensioned.

PETER MILLER came from Rowan county, North Carolina. He served in both the North and South Carolina troops and was in several battles. He settled in Anna township, Union county, Illinois, and died there. He is buried two miles north of Anna. "County History."

ELIAS MOIERS was from South Carolina, where he served in the war under Capt. William Williams and Col. William Polk for ten months. He was discharged on the "High Hills" of Santee, South Carolina. He came to Illinois, settling in Union county. In 1828 he applied for a pension stating that he was wholly disabled, that he did not ask for a pension sooner because he was able to work. He enumerated his possessions as one horse, one saddle, bridle and saddle bags. "Pension Records" and "County History."

TRAVIS MORRIS was born in Richmond county, Virginia, June 12, 1758. He enlisted for three months in 1777 with Capt. John Hedges and Col. Jesse Eural in the Virginia troops. Later he served in the North Carolina troops twice, for three months each with Capts. Charles Madden, Samuel Hampton and Major Joseph Winston. He came to Illinois and lived in both Alexander and Union counties. His place of burial is not known. He was pensioned.

JOHN MURPHY was from Burke county, North Carolina. He first fought with the Tories, but becoming convinced that the Continentals were in the right, he entered the army. After the war he came to Cape Girado, Missouri, then to Alexander county, Illinois and later to Union county settling in Anna township in 1816, where he died. "County History."

WILLIAM PARKS served in the war from Virginia and continued in the service after the close of the war. He came to Union county, Illinois, and is probably buried there.

WILLIAM SCOTT served in the war in the New York line of troops, enlisting when only sixteen years of age. He came to Illinois, residing in Union county, where he is probably buried. "County History."

JOHN SOWERS was born in Rowan county, North Carolina in 1760. He enlisted July, 1776, serving one month; again in 1781 in January, for three months, and again for the same time under Capt. John Lop. He came to Illinois, residing for a time in Adams county, but removed to Union county, where he died. He was pensioned.

JOSHUA VICK served in the war from Virginia. He removed to Tennessee and from there to Union county, Illinois, where he died. He was pensioned.

Vermilion County

The third of September, 1915, was a memorable day for the Gov. Bradford Chapter, D. A. R., of Danville. Several years ago the chapter decided to erect some fitting memorial to the memory of the soldiers of the American Revolution buried in Vermilion county. Plans crystallized into action and they decided to erect a drinking fountain. The design presented by Mr. Daniel French was accepted and the fountain complete was unveiled September 3, 1915.

The memorial consists of a floor thirty feet long, with seats at either end; a granite shaft eleven feet high holds in the center a bowl, into which water constantly flows. The shaft is ornamented near the top by a bronze wreath of laurel leaves, in which is the significant date, 1776. The granite shaft is superimposed with a four-foot bronze statue of a soldier of the Revolution standing at rest parade.

The names of the men are inscribed in the granite tablet set into the floor of the fountain. The inscription reads: "This statue is erected by the Daughters of the American Revolution in memory of the soldiers of the War for Independence who are buried in Vermilion county, Illinois." The chapter was most fortunate in having a "friend at court" in Hon. J. G. Cannon, who secured from the government an unused balance of money left from the erection of the government building, amounting to $6000, which was applied to erecting the shaft; the D. A. R. chapter being responsible for the bronze statue, costing $2000.

The program was as follows: Mrs. Daniel Hogan, regent of the chapter, presiding. "America," sung by "all the people," led by H. Y. Mercer, accompanied by the Soldiers' Home band. Invocation by Rev. George Howk Simonson. "Ritual of the Chapter," Mrs. James A. Meeks, chaplain. "Greetings," Mrs. W. E. Fithian. "Our Ancestors," Mr. W. R. Jewell. "Art in Bronze and Stone," Mr. James M. White, supervising architect of the University of Illinois.

"The Revolutionary War in the West," Dr. Otto L. Schmidt, president Illinois State Historical Society. Address, Hon. J. G. Cannon. Dedication and presentation of statue, Miss Lottie E. Jones, chairman Fountain Committee. Response, Gen. Frank S. Dickson, adjutant general, state of Illinois. The statue was unveiled by nine descendants of the men memorialized. Miss Lottie E. Jones deserves especial credit for the happy results of such strenuous labors, as she was the prime mover in the plans. The Soldiers' Home band furnished the music for the occasion. This is a most appropriate way to perpetuate the memory of brave men and brave deeds, since in the performing of such duties we promote a love of knowledge and intensify the patriotism of our people.

WILLIAM ADAMS was a native of Virginia, where he served in the war. After the war he removed to Kentucky. Coming to Illinois in 1825, he settled in Vermilion county, in Newell township, where he died, and is buried in the Martin burial ground. "Virginia Records."

DAVID BAIRD was born in New Jersey March 4, 1760. He enlisted in Monmouth county in the First New Jersey Militia, September, 1776. He re-enlisted, serving for different periods each year till the close of the war, serving under Capts. David Gordon, Kenneth Harrison, Coons, Samuel Carhart, John Price and Cornelius Schanck; Cols. Asher Holmes, Thomas Henderson and Cahart Walton. He served as private, sergeant, ensign, lieutenant and quartermaster. He came to Vermilion county to reside and died February 20, 1837; is buried in the Lebanon cemetery, Indianola. "New Jersey in the Revolution."

ROBERT BROWNFIELD was in the service in Pennsylvania with the Rangers. He came to Vermilion county, Illinois, and there applied for a pension. "Pennsylvania Archives" and "Pension Report."

JOSEPH COUGHRAN was born in Virginia January 16, 1761. He enlisted in June, 1781, in Hampshire county, with Capts. James Anderson, Alexander Dick and Isaac Parson, Col. Edwards, serving first four months and again for two months. After the war he came to Vermilion county, Illinois, where he applied for a pension in 1834. He died March 19, 1845. He is buried in Vermilion county, but the exact place is not known. He was pensioned.

KINZER DICKERSON was born in Maryland in 1757. He enlisted in the Pennsylvania line of troops in 1778, serving but one month under Col. Daniel Broadhead; he again served in 1779 for two months with Capt. Uriah Springer and Gen. Lachlen McIntosh. He again enlisted in 1782 for six weeks with Capt. John Crawford and Capt. J. Bean; again he served for one month with Capt. George Jenkins in Wheeling, Virginia. He came to Vermilion county, Illinois, to reside, where he applied for a pension, but having served less than six months it was not granted. "Pension Reports."

JOHN FRAZIER was a native of Virginia, where he served in the war, enlisting near the home of Laurence Washington. He served during the entire war and was present at the surrender of Cornwallis. The place of his burial is not known, but he died in Vermilion county. "Virginia Records."

JACOB GUNDY was born in Pennsylvania Oct. 13, 1759. He enlisted April, 1779, in Pennsylvania militia, under Capt. Sebastian Wolf and Quartermaster General Robert Patton, in Lancaster county, serving as a teamster for two months, and again for one month. After the war he removed to Ohio, and from there came to Vermilion county in 1830, with his son Joseph. He died in 1842, and is buried in the Gundy burying ground near Bismark. He was pensioned.

DANIEL HARRINGTON was born in Pennsylvania January 1, 1756. He enlisted in September, 1776, with Capt. Jacob Treck, Col. Michael Swope, in York county. He enlisted again, serving under the same officers, and a third time in Maryland with Capt. Daniel Shaw, Col. Edward Cockey, serving in all ten months. He came to Illinois, settling in Vermilion county, where he died in 1836. He was pensioned.

WILLIAM HARRIS served in the war from Pennsylvania. He came to Vermilion county, Illinois, and there applied for a pension, but not having served six months it was not granted. "Pennsylvania Archives" and "Pension Reports."

JAMES HULS was born in Virginia in 1761. He enlisted March 18, 1778, in the Fourth Virginia Regiment with Col. John Neville and Capt. John Stith, serving one year. He came to Vermilion county, Illinois, and died there in 1834. His widow drew his pension.

HUGH KING was born in North Carolina December 17, 1754. He enlisted in Mecklenburg county in 1778, re-enlisting twice, serving under Capts. John McRea and William Alexander, Major William Davis and Col. John Moore. He again enlisted in the South Carolina troops in 1781, serving with Capt. Andrew Alexander and Col. Wade Hampton in Washington's dragoons. In all he served seven times for a period of two years and ten months. He was in several skirmishes at Charlotte, North Carolina; Strawberry Fields, Quarter House and Ninety-six. He removed to Vermilion county, Illinois, where he died, and is buried in Springhill cemetery, Danville. He was pensioned.

THOMAS MAKEMSON was born in Pennsylvania in 1753. He enlisted with William Brown, commander of the Floating Battery, Putnam Station, twelve miles below Philadelphia. He served three years. Coming to Illinois, he located in Vermilion county, where he died in 1813, and is buried near Oakwood. He was pensioned.

THOMAS MORTON was born in Chester county, Pennsylvania, August 29, 1752. He enlisted three times, in 1775, 1776 and 1777, serving as ensign with Capts. James Elliott and James Lee, Col. Robert Culbertson. In 1780 he removed to Kentucky and served there with the Virginia troops as captain under Col. and Gen. George Rogers Clark. He was in skirmishes at Statton Island and with the Indians at Chillicothe. He came to Indiana, where he was appointed judge in Perry county in 1814. He removed to Vermilion county, Illinois, where he died. He was pensioned.

ZACHARIAH ROBERTSON, SR., was a soldier from Virginia, where he served in the war. He removed to Harrison county, Kentucky, and in 1834 came to Vermilion county, Illinois, settling in Newell township. He died on the land where Bismarck now stands, at the advanced age of 94 years. "Virginia Records."

Wabash County

JOHN ARMSTRONG came from North Carolina, where he served in the war. He removed to Kentucky, and from there to Tennessee, and in 1815 he came to Wabash county, settling on the land purchased of Levi Compton, where he died. "North Carolina Records" and "County History."

ROBERT BELL was born in the north of Ireland. He came to America and enlisted when only sixteen years of age, serving in the light artillery under Lafayette in the Virginia line of troops. He came from Rockbridge county, Virginia, to Wabash county, Illinois, in 1818, settling in Friendsville precinct, where he died in 1837. "Virginia Records" and "County History."

WILLIAM DOUGHTON served in the Virginia line of troops. He came to Wabash county, Illinois, in 1820, from West Virginia. He died December 1, 1833. He was pensioned.

JOHN GORDON was born in Wheeling, West Virginia, in 1763. He served in the war from that state. Coming to Ohio, he removed to Indiana, and in 1819 he came to Lawrence county, Illinois, but in 1829 he lived in Mt. Carmel, Wabash county, where he died. "Virginia Records" and "County History."

JONATHAN GOSS was from Massachusetts, where he served under Capt. John Minot, Col. Josiah Whitney's regiment, from May, 1777, to July. He came to Illinois and resided in Wabash county, where he died, and is buried in Friendsville. He was pensioned.

HEZEKIAH HARDESTY was born September 2, 1763, on the eastern shore of Maryland. He served six times—March, 1778, one month; May, 1778, two months; September, 1778, four months; April, 1779, one month; October, 1780, one month; May, 1782, one month. He was under Ensign Charles Goodwin and Capts. David Owen, Joseph Cross, Ruble and Joseph Bean, and with Col. William McFarlan and Gen. Lochlan McIntosh and William Crawford in Pennsylvania troops. He came to Lawrence county, Illinois, but for a time resided in Fulton county, returning to Lawrence county. He is buried near Allendale, Wabash county. He died after 1829. He was pensioned.

NATHANIEL HENDRYX came from New York, where he served in the war. He was in the Albany county militia, in the Seventeenth regiment. After the war he removed to Wabash county, Illinois, where he probably died as he was an aged man before he applied for a pension. He was pensioned.

JOHN HUNTER served in the Virginia troops under Capt. James Gray in Company 2, in 1778. Coming to Illinois, he settled in Wabash county, where he applied for a pension, but not having served six months it was not granted. "Virginia Records."

PETER KEEN was from New Jersey, where he served in the war. He removed to Ohio, and in 1814 came to Wabash county, Illinois, and was one of the original proprietors of Palmyra, and later moved to Friendsville, where he died in

1840. "New Jersey Records" and "County History."

WILLIAM LAWSON was from Scott county, Virginia. He served in the Virginia troops. He came to Wabash county, Illinois, and there applied for a pension. He was pensioned.

THOMAS PULLIAM served in the war from Virginia. He came to Wabash county, Illinois, in 1815, settling in the town of Coffee. "Virginia Records."

STEPHEN SOMMERS was from Connecticut, where he enlisted July 3, 1781, in the First Regiment, commanded by Col. John Durkee. He was born in 1762. He came to Wabash county, Illinois, at an early date, and died there. He was pensioned.

ALEXANDER STEWART was from New Jersey, where he served in both the Continental Army and the militia. He came to Wabash county to reside. The place of burial is not known. He was pensioned.

JOHN STILLWELL was from Virginia, where he served in the war. He came to Wabash county, Illinois, in 1820, settling in the town of Belmont, where he died. "Virginia Records" and "County History."

THOMAS THOMPSON was in the Virginia line of troops. He came to Wabash county, Illinois, and died there January 19, 1829. He was pensioned.

ANDREW TUTTLE was from Connecticut. He served in the war in Col. Samuel Crawford's regiment from Milford, enlisting September,

1781. He came to Wabash county, Illinois, and is doubtless buried there. He was pensioned.

JOHN WHITE was born in Stafford, Connecticut, May 7, 1761. He enlisted four times, first in 1776 for three months; in 1777 for six months; in 1778 for six months, and the same year for three months. He served under Capt. Abner Robinson. He came to Wabash county, Illinois, and died there September 2, 1834. He was pensioned.

JOHN WOOD was from Maryland, where he served as ensign in the war. He removed to Wabash county, Illinois, and died there November 4, 1832, and was buried in the Newkirk cemetery, near Friendsville. He made the first permanent settlement in 1809, coming from Kentucky, he brought apple trees from which originated the "Wood Apple." He also built Fort Wood. He was pensioned.

Warren County

JAMES MEADOWS was born in Virginia in 1750. While a young man he went to North Carolina to reside and entered the service from that state. He served until the close of the war. In 1794 he removed to Kentucky, and in 1832 came to Illinois to reside, settling in Warren county. His grave in the Meridan cemetery was marked by the Puritan and Cavalier Chapter, D. A. R., of Monmouth. "Virginia Records."

Washington County

GEORGE BROWN was from Virginia, born in Chesterfield county in 1752. He enlisted in Charlotte county March, 1780, serving two months with Capt. Thomas Williams; again in 1781 for two months under Capt. Dudley Barrel and Col. Peter Muhlenberg; again he served for two months under Capt. Pickeway and Col. Holt Richardson. He removed to Washington county, Illinois, where he died March 24, 1842. He was pensioned.

JAMES CRABTREE was from Virginia, where he served in the war as ensign in the Washington county line of troops. He came to Washington county, Illinois, and died there. He was pensioned.

CONRAD GOODNER was from North Carolina, and served from that state. He came to Illinois, settling in St. Clair county, but removed to Washington county, where he died. He was pensioned.

THOMAS McCLERKEN was from Chester county, Camden district, South Carolina. He removed to Kentucky, and from there to Indiana, and thence to Washington county, Illinois, where he died, and is buried near Sparta. A stone tells of his being a Revolutionary soldier. Each year the Grand Army post places flowers on his grave. At the age of 95 years he applied for a pension, but doubtless died before it was granted. "County and Family Histories."

Wayne County

JAMES CLARK was born April 18, 1755, in Rowan county, North Carolina. He enlisted in South Carolina August 1, 1776, serving one year under Capt. John Gowens. He again enlisted for four months with Capt. John Earle; again he served from October, 1777, to July, 1778, as first lieutenant, and again from July, 1780, to June, 1781, and again in 1781 for nine months, all under Capts. William Wood, John Nesbit, Samuel Earle, Henry Wood and James McIllhaney, with Col. John Thomas. Once more this intrepid soldier served his country for three months from June, 1782, and was made captain, and again for one month from August, 1782, making in all seven enlistments. He was wounded in the thigh at Hiamassee and Blackstock's. He removed to Kentucky in 1801, and in 1818 came to Wayne county, Illinois, where he died August 25, 1834. He was pensioned.

GEORGE CLARK served in the war from Virginia. After the war he removed to Kentucky, and from there to Gallatin county, Illinois, but died in Wayne county very aged. He was pensioned.

JAMES GASTON was born in Lancaster county, South Carolina, July 24, 1761. He enlisted in 1778 with Capt. John Marshall; was taken prisoner and confined in Camden jail for two months. He was paroled, then enlisted again under Capt. William Ingram, also served under Capt. Nisbet, serving until May, 1781. He was in the battle of Hanging Rock. He removed to Indiana, and from there to Wayne county, Illinois, where he died at Fairfield March 7, 1840. He was the first person to be buried in Bovee cemetery. He was one of nine sons of John Gaston to serve in the war. "South Carolina Records" and "County History."

JOHN HANSON was born in Virginia about 1761, where he enlisted in 1778 for two months under Capt. Evans Shelby. He again served in 1781 for ten months with Capt. John McIlhaney and Col. Hammond in the North Carolina troops. He removed to Indiana, and from there to Wayne county, Illinois, where he died July 25, 1835. He was pensioned.

JAMES LOCK was from Virginia, born in Berkeley county August 24, 1761. He enlisted in 1779 for three months with Capt. Samuel McCutchen and Col. William Bone. He again served in 1781 for three months with Capt. John McCormick and Col. William Darke. He removed to Wayne county, Illinois, where he is doubtless buried. He was pensioned.

JOHN H. MILLS was from the Carolinas and served in the war from South Carolina. He came to Wayne county, Illinois, and was still living in 1840, aged 87 years. He applied for a pension, but doubtless died before it was granted. His name was given by the marshal of the district. "Pension Record" and "County History."

WILLIAM SIMPSON was born in Prince William county, Virginia, October 14, 1755, and served in the Virginia troops. He removed to Wayne county, Illinois, and died there in 1839. He was pensioned.

THOMAS SLOAN served in the war from North Carolina. After the war he came to Illinois, settling in McLean county, but removed to Wayne county, where he died. He was pensioned.

JAMES STUART was born in South Carolina December 1, 1762, where he enlisted in 1779 for two months with Capt. H. McClure and Col. E. Lacey. He enlisted again in 1780 for three months, serving with Capt. John McClure; again he served the same year under Capts. John Steele and Philip Walker, and twice more, making five enlistments, under Col. E. Lacey. He was in the battles of Rocky Creek, Hanging Rock, King's Mountain, Fort Granby, siege of Ninety-six, Haddrell's Point and Eutaw Springs. He removed to Kentucky, and from there to Wayne county, Illinois, where he died October, 1845, in Fairfield township. He was pensioned.

White County

DANIEL BIDWELL served in the war from New York in the Albany county militia, Thirteenth Regiment, with Capt. John McCrea. He removed to White county, Illinois, and died there. He was pensioned.

JOHN CHILDRESS served in the war from North Carolina. He came to Illinois, settling in Carmi, White county, where he probably died. He was pensioned.

THOMAS DAGLEY probably served in the war from North Carolina. He came to White county, Illinois, and died there. He lies buried in the Union Ridge cemetery, about ten miles south of Carmi. "Family Records."

HEZEKIAH DAVIS was from South Carolina, where he served in the war. He came to Illinois about 1811 and was living in Jackson county, but removed to White county, and died there in 1820. He was wounded in the service. He was pensioned.

CLEMENT EDERLIN was from Maryland, where he served as sergeant in the First Regiment in 1776 with Capt. John Haskins and Col. William Smallwood. He removed to Kentucky, and from there to White county, Illinois. He is buried in the Morris cemetery, White county. He was pensioned.

EDMOND FEAR was in the war from Virginia. He came to White county, Illinois, and there applied for a pension, but not having served six months it was not granted. "Virginia Records" and "Pension Report."

SAMUEL HALE served in the war from Virginia. Coming to Illinois he settled in White county and there applied for a pension. He died in 1849, aged 98 years. "Virginia Records" and "County History."

JOSEPH HAWTHORNE served in the war from South Carolina. He came to White county, Illinois, and died there. He was buried in the Enfield cemetery. He was pensioned.

ROBERT HAWTHORNE was doubtless a brother of Joseph, and he also served from South Carolina. He came to White county, Illinois, and died there. He was buried in the Enfield cemetery. He was pensioned.

WILLIAM HOOD served as ensign in Capt. James Calderwood's company, Col. Daniel Morgan's regiment of Virginia troops, from May 31, 1777, to November 30, 1778. He came to White county, Illinois, and died there in 1827. He was pensioned.

NATHAN JAGGERS was born October 16, 1759, in Craven county, South Carolina. He enlisted October, 1775, for three months with Capt. Edmund Strange; again in 1779 for three months with Capt. John Nixon, Col. John Winn, in the South Carolina troops. He again enlisted in 1780, serving more than one year with Capts. Thomas Taylor, George Hastin, Shaw and Kirkwood, with Col. Edward Lacy, in the Virginia troops. He again served from February, 1782, for two months under Capt. Neeley and Col. Edward Lacey, and also Col. McDonald in the South Carolina troops. He came to White county, Illinois, where he died August 19, 1839. He was pensioned.

ARTHUR JOHNSON was born August 7, 1757, in Brunswick county, Virginia. He served as corporal in Capt. James Knox's company, Col. Abraham Bowman's Eighth Regiment, from May, 1776, to April 30, 1777. He again enlisted January 2, 1777, for three years. He was in Capt. Thomas Berry's company, Eighth Regiment, serving as sergeant; also with Capt. Abraham Kirkpatrick's company, same regiment. He was acting sergeant in Capt. William Crogan's company, Fourth Regiment, and in May, 1779, in Capt. Leonard Cooper's company with Col. John Nevill's Fourth Regiment. After the war he removed to Kentucky, and from there to Indiana, Gibson county, and later to White county, Illinois, where he died October 16, 1839, and was buried in the Seven Mile Prairie cemetery, four miles north of Enfield. A monument has been erected by descendants, upon which is inscribed his military record. "Virginia Records."

CHARLES KNIGHT was from Virginia, where he served in the war. He came to White county, Illinois, and died there. He lies buried in the Union Ridge cemetery, about ten miles south of Carmi. "Virginia Records."

HENRY MORGAN was born in North Carolina December 7, 1758. He enlisted March 24, 1779, for five months with Capt. Robert. McLane and Col. John Collier; in August, 1780, he served one month with Capt. Flower Swift and Col. William Campbell in the Virginia troops. In

1781 he served one year and six months with Capt. Robert McLane and Major Joel Paisley in the North Carolina troops. He was in the battles of Wetzell's Mills, Sandy Creek and Lindley's Mill. He removed to White county, Illinois, and died there February 22, 1849. He was pensioned.

MATHIAS PARR was from New York, where he served in the war in the Second Regiment, New York troops, under Col. Philip Van Courtland. He was born in 1746. Coming to Illinois, he settled in Fayette county, but removed to White county, where he died at an advanced age. He was pensioned.

JOHN SCARBOROUGH was born in April, 1762, in Virginia. He enlisted in 1780, serving until April 4, 1781, under Capts. Samuel Selden and James Green. He again enlisted, serving until June, 1783, when he was discharged, serving with Capt. John Hughes and Col. Anthony White. He came to Indiana, and from there to Franklin county, Illinois, and later to White county, where he died August 15, 1846. He was pensioned.

PETER SHOLL was a native of Pennsylvania, where he enlisted in the Northampton county militia, first company, under Capt. Adam Stohler, third battalion, and Col. Michael Pabst in 1778. He removed to White county, Illinois, and died at an advanced age. He was pensioned.

WILLIAM STEWART was born in Mecklenburg county, North Carolina, in 1763. He enlisted in 1780 under Col. John Patton and was wounded at the battle of Camden. He came to White county, Illinois, and died there in 1856.

He lies buried in the old cemetery at Paxton, White county. "North Carolina Records."

JOHN THOMPSON served from Virginia. He came to Indiana and was pensioned there in 1833. Coming to White county, Illinois, to reside, he died in the county. He was pensioned.

ELIAS VEATH or VEACH was from Pendleton county, South Carolina. He served in the war from that state. He came to Illinois and settled in White county, where at the age of 74 he applied for a pension. He was pensioned. His widow drew a pension after his death.

Whiteside County

ALEXANDER THOMPSON was born in Cumberland county, Pennsylvania, in 1758. He enlisted August, 1776, for two months with Capt. Alexander Laughlin and Col. William Clark. He again enlisted in December for the same time and with the same officers. He served again under Col. Arthur Buchanan, all in the Pennsylvania line of troops. He removed to Indiana, and later to Whiteside county, Illinois, where he died at Newton September 25, 1840. He was pensioned.

Will County

EBENEZER COLLINS was born in New York. He enlisted with Capt. Solomon Wadsworth in the Third Company, Fifth Regiment, called the Van Veghten Regiment. He came to Illinois, settling in Will county. He is probably buried in Homer township. "New York in the Revolution."

JOHN COOK was born in Hanover, Morris county, New Jersey, December 25, 1761. He enlisted August, 1776, serving two years in the companies of Capts. David Bates, Obadiah Kitchell, Elijah Squire, Benjamin Corey, William Ely, John Scudder, Levi Gardiner, Harrison Baldwin, Lewis Brant and David Lyon with Cols. Benoni Hathaway, Ellis Cook, Sylvanus Seeley and Moses Jacques in the New Jersey troops. He came to reside in Will county, Illinois, where he died near Joliet, October 24, 1837, and is buried in Oakwool cemetery, Joliet. "New Jersey in the Revolution."

CHARLES DENNEY was a native of New York, born in Pauldingstown, Dutchess county, December 25, 1759. He enlisted in the summer of 1777 and served nine months under Capts. Noah Wheeler and Seth Wheeler with Col. Roswell Hopkins in the New York troops. He came to Will county, Illinois, settling near Joliet, where he died August 6, 1839, aged 79 years, and is buried at Mokena, Will county. "New York in the Revolution."

WILLIAM HEWES was born in Attlebury, Massachusetts, in 1761, he enlisted in June, 1780, serving five months under Capts. Caleb Robinson and Nehemiah Houghton with Col. George Reid in the New Hampshire troops. He came to Illinois to reside and died in Crete, Illinois, Will county, in 1855. "New Hampshire in the Revolution."

Williamson County

JOHN CHANDOIN was from Virginia, born in 1759. He served in the Virginia troops. Coming to Illinois, he settled in Franklin county, but died in Williamson county, which was formed from Franklin. He was pensioned.

ARCHIBALD DANIEL came from Wilmington, Bladen county, North Carolina. He served in the war from that state. Coming to Illinois, he settled in Franklin county, but removed to Gallatin county, and from there to Williamson county, where he died in 1844. He was pensioned.

BENJAMIN GILL served in the war from North Carolina. He was shot through the ear and was thought to be dead. After the war he removed to Williamson county, Illinois, where he died. "County History."

BENAIJAH GILL served in the war from New Jersey. He came to Williamson county, Illinois, where he died. He was pensioned.

MOSES JONES was from North Carolina. He served in Capt. Benjamin Bailey's company, North Carolina troops, in the Tenth Regiment, from September 10, 1782, until March 1, 1783. He came to Illinois in 1819, settling in Franklin county, but died in Williamson county, northern precinct. He was pensioned.

JOHN G. LUMPKINS was from Pittsylvania county, Virginia. He served in the Virginia line of troops. He came to Illinois, settling in Williamson county, where he applied for a pension. "Pension Reports of 1840" and "Virginia Records."

ABEL MANN served in the Virginia troops. Coming to Illinois, he settled in Franklin county, but died in Williamson county. He was pensioned.

JOSEPH NEWTON was born in North Carolina in 1760. In 1776 he served as a substitute and was in the battles of Cowpens and Guilford

Court House. He came to Illinois about 1815, settling in Pope county. He removed to Williamson county, where he died in 1842. "Pension Records."

JOHN PAINTER served in the Virginia troops, and was paid off at Romney. He came to Williamson county, Illinois, and died there. He was pensioned.

PHILIP RUSSELL served in the Virginia troops and was present when Cornwallis surrendered. He carried a bullet in his body during his life. He removed to Tennessee, and in 1817 came to Franklin county, but died in Williamson county on the farm owned by W. Hindeman. He was pensioned.

JOHN ROBINSON was born in South Carolina in 1750. He enlisted four times, first in 1776 for three months with Capt. John Lyles and Col. James Lyles; he served three months in 1777 under the same officers; again served three months in 1781 with Capt. Jeremiah Williams and Col. Samuel Hammond. He was in several engagements with the Cherokee Indians. He lived in Franklin county, Illinois, but died in Williamson county July 20, 1835. He was pensioned.

JOHN G. SIMPKINS was born in 1756, probably in New York state. He enlisted in New York in 1777, serving until 1781 under Capt. John Rudolph and Col. Henry Lee in the Continental Dragoons. He was discharged in South Carolina. He removed to Franklin county, Illinois, but lived in Vigo county, Indiana, then back to Franklin county, but died in Williamson county July 22, 1843. He was pensioned.

Winnebago County

SAMUEL CAMPBELL was a native of Massachusetts, born Oct. 8, 1762. He was a private in Capt. John Spoor's company, Col. John Brown's regiment, serving three months and seven days with Col. John Ashley Jr.'s regiment. Again under Lieut. Moses Hubbard by order of Gen. John Fellows, and with Capt. James Campbell, service six days. Samuel Campbell came to Illinois and settled in Winnebago county, where he died Nov. 8, 1844, and is buried in the Hulse cemetery Pecatonica. His grave was marked May 26, 1908. "Massachusetts in the Revolution."

JEHIEL HARMON was born in Suffield, Connecticut, Oct. 5, 1762. He early enlisted in the service of his country, taking the place of an older brother who was ill and forced to leave the service. His service was during the closing six months of the war. He came to Illinois and settled in Winnebago county, where he died March 3, 1845, and is buried in the West Side cemetery, Rockford. His grave was marked June 14 1902. "Connecticut in the Revolution."

EPHRIAM PALMER was a native of Massachusetts; he enlisted in 1777 when but 17 years of age in Capt. Sylvanus Cobb's company, for one month, and again for three months with the same leader. In 1778 and 1779 he served one year in Capt. Samuel Lockwood's company, Col. John Wood's Regiment. He was taken prisoner June 7, 1779, and confined in the Small Pox Hospital, New York; was exchanged February, 1780, and again served his country, enlisting from Salem, New York, as a substitute with Capt. Wm. Stevens, and was one who was placed to guard the notorious Major Andre. He early came to Illinois, settling in Winnebago county, where he died and is buried in the Kishwaukee cemetery, Kishwaukee. His grave was marked in June, 1907. "Massachusetts in the Revolution."

Woodford County

EDWARD FITZPATRICK was born in Ireland in 1760. He came to America when a boy. He entered the service as a private in Capt. John Armstrong's company, North Carolina troops. Coming to Illinois he settled in what is now Woodford county in 1832. He died there Nov. 21, 1834, and is buried in the Fitzpatrick cemetery near Leon. "North Carolina in the Revolution."

BASIL MEEK was born in Virginia, March 7, 1763. He served in Capt. Hugh Stevenson's company from August, 1775, to October. He came to Illinois, settling in what is now Woodford county, in 1832. He died Jan. 12, 1844, and is buried in Olio township cemetery, near Eureka. A fine monument has been erected to his memory. The graves of both Edward Fitzpatrick and Basil Meek were marked by the Peoria Chapter D. A. R., assisted by the Historical Society of Woodford county. A most interesting program was given, consisting of an address by the Hon. J. V. Graff, and by the state regent, Mrs. George T. Page. "Virginia Records."

CHARLES MOORE was born in Hanover county, Virginia, Jan. 11, 1763. He enlisted from Salisbury district, Rowan county, North Carolina, serving three months, in Capt. James Craig's company, and Major Montflorance's regiment. He again served three months in Capt.

Benjamin Smith's company, Col. Matthew Brandon's regiment, serving six months; also in Capt. Robert Gladsby's company. He was in the battle of King's mountain. He came to Illinois, settling in Sangamon county near Buffalo Hart Grove, in 1823, but moved to what is now Woodford county. While going to draw his pension the stage upset and from injuries received he died Sept. 19, 1839. He is probably buried in Woodford county. He was pensioned. "Family Records."

INDEX

INDEX

Abney, William	42
Adams, William	157
Allen, Archibald	120
Allen, Eleazer	144
Allen, William	42
Allere, Bazelle	129
Allere, Joseph	130
Anderson, Joseph	122
Antere, Michael	129
Archer, Zachariah	18
Armstrong, John	161
Ashe, Thomas	88
Austin, Elijah	31
Baker, Absalom	77
Baker, Isaac	132
Baker, Michael M.	45
Baird, David	157
Baith, George	25
Baldwin, David	53
Banes, John	117
Banow, Daniel	57
Barbau, Jean Baptiste, Sr.	130
Barker, Jacob	50
Barker, Zebediah	100
Barnes, Ebenezer	93
Barr, Hugh	31
Barrack, Peter	25
Bartholomew, Joseph	94
Bartlett, Ebenezer	18
Bates, William	58
Bean, Nicholas	18
Beard, James	67
Beaulieu, Michael	150
Beckwith, Silas	25
Beeler, Capt. Samuel	94
Beer, Robert	39
Beggs, Alexander	152
Bell, Robert	161
Bell, Nathaniel	144
Beman, William	46
Bennett, William	63
Benson, James	31
Bettisworth, Charles	53
Bidwell, Daniel	168
Bienvenue, Antoine Sr.	129
Biggs, Elijah	143
Biggs, William	78
Bivens, John	41
Blair, David	141
Blair, William	141
Blankenship, Benjamin	54
Blouin, Daniel	129
Bobbitt, Ishmail	109
Boismenue, M.	145
Bond, Shadrach Sr.	100
Boon, Thomas	19
Borders, Peter	72
Bostwick, Ezra	104
Bourn, Ebenezer	100
Boutwell, Stephen	42
Brady, Thomas	144
Brady, Mrs. Thomas	145
Bratney, Robert	124
Breckman, Thomas	104
Briance, Henry	104
Bridges, Allen J.	46
Bridges, George	78
Briscoe, Henry	19
Broadwell, Moses	133
Bromlet, Reuben	130
Bronson, Phineas	115
Brown, Daniel	79
Brown, George	11
Brown, George	164
Brown, Nathan	63
Brown, Samuel	73
Bromfield, Robert	16
Brownfield, Robert	158
Bryan, George	133
Bruner, Adam	65
Bruner, Peter	65
Burnham, Gurdin	32
Burroughs, Daniel	63
Burris, Martin	109
Burton, John	133
Busby, Robert	73
Byrum, Benjamin	122
Caldwell, Samuel	53
Callis, David	117
Campbell, Enos	134
Campbell, Samuel	176
Cannady, John	105
Carnelison, John	79
Carpenter, Benjamin	141
Carrigan, John	20
Carr, Joseph	145
Carver, Christian	134
Cassady, William	140
Cavaley, A. W.	141
Cesire, Antoine	150
Cesire, Joseph	150
Chafin, Elias	20
Chandler, Daniel	59
Chandoin, John	173
Chapman, Daniel	61
Chapin, Samuel	55
Charleville, Jean Baptiste	130
Chase, Parker	30
Cheshier, James	36
Childers, Isham	68
Childress, John	168
Choate, Greenberry	43
Christian, Daniel	15
Clapp, Adam	11
Clark, Bazel (Barzilla)	134
Clark, George	166

Clark, James	165	Dubois, Toussaint	68
Clark, John	46	Dubuque, Jean Baptiste	150
Clarkson, Constantine	109	Dudley, John	30
Clay, Elijah	32	Duff, John	43
Clendenin, John	123	Duncan, John	20
Clifford, Michael	135	Dunn, Charles	119
Cline, Jonas	39	Dunlap, William	26
Collins, Ebenezer	172	Dusenberry, John	115
Collins, Henry	67	Ebelin, Samuel	88
Collinsworth, John	145	Ederlin, Clement	168
Collom, Jonathan	22	Edgar, Capt. John	124
Conner, Samuel	9	Edwards, Joseph	152
Conn, John	145	Ellis, John	153
Conrey, John	32	Ellsworth, John	95
Conway, Jesse	46	Evans, John	120
Cook, John	172	Evans, Joseph	36
Cooper, Jonathan	59	Fear, Edmond	169
Cotton, John	9	Fee, John	9
Cottingham, George	22	Fellows, Willis	26
Couch, Mellington	122	Ferguson, Lewis	97
Coughran, Joseph	158	Files, John	35
Covell, Henry	9	Finn, Peter	88
Coy, Christopher	68	Finley, David	55
Crabtree, James	165	Fisk, Robert	136
Crabtree, John	105	Fitzgerald, George	51
Craig, Thomas	105	Fitzpatrick, Edward	177
Creed, Colbay	15	Flatt, John	47
Crose, Philip	94	Foster, Abner	43
Crow, William	115	Fowler, William	125
Crowder, Philip	135	Frazier, John	158
Crutcher, Henry	129	French, John	73
Curry, James	123	Friatt, Robert	57
Curry, Nicholas	142	Frick, Jacob	153
Cutright, Peter	30	Frizzell, Earl	55
Dagley, Thomas	168	Frost, Joseph	23
Daniel, Archibald	174	Fry, Robert	57
Danis, Jerome	129	Gannon, William Sr.	32
Danis, Joseph	129	Gardner, Samuel	38
Danis, Michael	129	Garretson, James	101
Davis, Aquilla	135	Garrison, James	47
Davis, Grandfather	50	Gaston, James	166
Davis, Hezekiah	168	Gaston, William	88
Day, Daniel	114	Gaylord, Lemuel	90
Day, Edward	29	Gibbs, Truman	69
Dawson, John	109	Gilbert, Ashael	65
Deck, Michael	79	Gill, Benajiah	174
Denison, William	68	Gill, Benjamin	174
Denney, Charles	173	Gill, Thomas	26
Devoir, Luke	119	Gillham, Isaac	80
Diamond, John	12	Gillham, James	81
Dickey, William	73	Gillham, John	81
Dickerson, Kinzer	158	Gillham, Thomas	81
Dingman, James	135	Gillham, William	59
Dodge, John	123	Gilmore, Huriah	73
Dolahide, Francis	50	Ginger, Henry	37
Dollar, William	40	Giradin, Antoine	150
Dortch, Abel	38	Giradot, Piere	101
Doughton, William	161	Glenn, John	69
Doyle, John	124	Glover, Benjamin	119
Dozier, Peter	19	Godin, Michael	130

Godin, Turanjeau	151	Howard, John	40
Goodner, Conrad	165	Howard, William	101
Gordon, Benjamin	106	Howell, Lewis	131
Gordon, Jesse	57	Hubbard, Peter	12
Gordon, John	161	Hudson, Samuel	82
Goss, Jonathan	161	Huls, James	159
Gray, Elliot	151	Hunter, John	162
Greene, Henry	141	Hurst, William	32
Griffiths, William	40	Jackson, Joseph	110
Griswold, Adonijah	47	Jackson, Samuel	110
Gundy, Jacob	159	Jaggers, Nathan	169
Hadden, Elisha	22	James, Thomas	137
Haggard, David	95	James, William	33
Haggard, James	136	Janis, Nicholas	130
Haile, William	136	Jenkins, Job	110
Hainline, George Sr.	42	Jenkins, John	143
Hale, Samuel	169	Johnson, Arthur	170
Hall, William	81	Johnson, Benjamin	83
Hamilton, Thomas	130	Johnson, Hugh	20
Hancock, Bennet	43	Johnson, Moses	17
Hancock, Daniel	120	Jolly, Boling	110
Haney, Francis	59	Jones, Joseph	146
Hanson, John	166	Jones, Moses	174
Hapsonstall, Abraham	66	Jones, Samuel	111
Hardesty, Hezekiah	162	Jones, Stephen	10
Hargrave, John	153	Jones, William	137
Harkness, James	116	Jordan, James	111
Harmon, Jehiel	176	Justus, Moses	92
Harris, William	159	Karr, John C.	96
Harris, Wooten	106	Keen, Peter	162
Harrison, Anthony A.	82	Kehr, David	118
Harrison, Ezekiel	136	Keller, Isaac	23
Harrington, Daniel	159	Kendrick, William	14
Harrington, John	66	Kenney, Daniel	26
Harrolson, Paul	125	Kennison, David	24
Hart, John	23	Kidd, Robert	101
Hart, Thomas	13	Killebrue, Lawrence	111
Harwick, Jacob	61	Kimes, Henry	72
Hawthorne, Joseph	169	Kincaid, Samuel	69
Hawthorne, Robert	169	Kincaid, Samuel	27
Hays, William	16	Kincaid, Thomas	27
Henderson, Wilson	44	King, Hugh	159
Hendryx, Nathaniel	162	King, John	20
Hester, Ferrel	32	Kirby, William	16
Hewes, William	173	Kitchen, James	40
Hewitt, John	47	Klepinger, Adam	27
Hicklin, Jonathan	17	Knight, Charles	170
Highsmith, Benjamin	69	Knight, James Sr.	33
Hiltebrand, John	125	Knighten, Thomas	146
Hilton, Andrew	101	Lackey, Adam	69
Hix, David	125	La Croix, Jean Baptiste	151
Hoar, David	125	Lamb, John Sr.	44
Hobart, Jonas	92	Lambert, Joseph	146
Hodge, Francis	95	Land, Moses	21
Hood, William	169	Langston, William	91
Hooker, John	38	Lanman, James	141
Horner, Nicholas	145	Latimer, Jonathan	66
Houghton, Aaron	98	Lathrop, Isaac	19
Houghman, Moses	95	Lavigne, Antoine	129
House, Elias	153	Lawson, John	125

Name	Page	Name	Page
Lawson, Randolph	62	McWithey, James	118
Lawson, William	163	Meadows, James	164
Layton, Thomas	19	Meadows, William	34
Leman, James	101	Means, William	34
Levens, Henry Sr.	102	Meek, Basil	177
Lewis, John	17	Meisenhimer, Peter	154
Lewis, Timothy	13	Melton, Benjamin	70
Liget, John	106	Melton, William	70
Lipe, Leonard	117	Miller, Francis	48
Lipsiè, John	54	Miller, John A.	48
Little, Samuel	60	Miller, Michael	102
Lively, John	125	Miller, Peter	154
Lock, James	167	Millington, Peter	138
Lockridge, John	137	Mills, Haydon	126
Logue, Thomas	102	Mills, John H.	167
Long, James	12	Minzes, Joseph	38
Long, John	83	Mizner, Henry	64
Long, William	60	Mitchell, Rev. Edward	147
Looker, Othniel	27	Mitchell, James	147
Lorton, Robert	48	Mitchell, Rev. Samuel	61
Lucas, Abram	137	Montgomery, John	116
Luke, Thomas	70	Montgomery, John	126
Lumpkins, John G.	174	Moiers, Elias	154
Lunsford, George	102	Moody, Edmund	111
Luttrell, Michael	89	Moore, Andrew	120
Lyerle, Christopher	153	Moore, Asa	34
Lynn, David	55	Moore, Charles	177
Lyrely, Zachariah	58	Moore, Capt. James	102
Maillet, Paulette	116	Moore, Risdon	146
Makemson, Thomas	160	Moore, Thomas	74
Mallory, Samuel	40	Moore, Thomas L.	21
Manley, David	66	Morrell, John	37
Mann, Abel	174	Morris, Travis	154
Martin, John	10	Morrison, Joseph	89
Massie, Thomas	137	Moss, Zealy	116
Matteson, Thomas	31	Morgan, Henry	170
Mather, Elihu	83	Morton, Thomas	160
Maulding, Ambrose	51	Murray, Daniel	126
Mayberry, Frederick	51	Murphy, John	60
Mayfield, John	74	Murphy, John	117
Maxcy, Joel	138	Murphy, John	154
McAdams, Joseph	12	Myers, William	21
McAdams, William	83	Nance, Zachariah	98
McClerkin, Thomas	165	Neer, Jacob	12
McClintock, Samuel	151	Newton, Joseph	174
McClure, Samuel	19	Nixon, George	56
McClure, Thomas	96	Norton, James	44
McCullough, William	96	O'Flyng, Patrick	111
McDaniel, Randle	52	Ogden, Stephen	34
McElyea, William	38	Ogle, Joseph	147
McEvers, James	142	Olmsted, Joseph	118
McGahy, David	28	Outhouse, Peter	21
McGhee, William	96	Overstreet, John	98
McMahon, Constantine	28	Owens, Mason	107
McMillan, Daniel	56	Pace, Joel	60
McNab, Charles	126	Paddock, Gaius	84
McNary, Hugh	118	Padfield, William	147
McNeely, David	120	Pagan, David	126
McPeters, David	111	Painter, John	175
McRoberts, James	102	Painter, Joseph	23

Palmer, Ephraim	176
Parker, John	24
Parks, Samuel	17
Parks, William	155
Parr, Mathias	171
Patterson, Alexander K.	54
Patterson, James	108
Patterson, Solomon	142
Patton, Thomas	28
Peake, John	138
Peebles, John	74
Peltier, Joseph	151
Penny, William	139
Perkins, Rufus	114
Perkins, Ute	54
Perrin, Nathaniel	118
Phelps, Rufus	115
Phillips, David	148
Piper, Asa	28
Piggott, James	148
Pillars, James	126
Pillars, Richard	126
Pinkstaff, Andrew	70
Pixley, Job	36
Plant, Williamson	13
Posey, Gen. Thomas	44
Post, Caleb	49
Powers, Abner	63
Prickett, George	84
Prime, or Primm, John	148
Proctor, Little Page	52
Proctor, Nicholas	52
Pruitt, Martin	84
Pulliam, George	139
Pulliam, John	148
Pulliam, Thomas	163
Purvines, John	139
Pyatt, Ebenezer	58
Ralls, Rawleigh	127
Ralston, William	139
Randle, Isham	85
Randle, Richard	85
Randleman, Martin	149
Redmon, George	34
Redmon, Samuel	149
Reed, Charles	71
Revis, Harris	107
Revis, Henry	85
Rhodes, Daniel	34
Richard, Joseph	130
Richards, William	86
Richardson, James	107
Richardson, Joshua	74
Richardson, Thomas	49
Riggs, Hosea	149
Ritchey, John	40
Roach, Francis	86
Roark, William	131
Roberts, John	129
Roberts, Thomas	112
Robertson, John	112
Robertson, Zachariah	160
Robinson, James	71
Robinson, John	74
Robinson, John	175
Rogers, John	71
Rogers, Peter	103
Rogers, William	38
Roper, George	89
Rose, Richard	54
Ross, Reuben	74
Rowe, Hezekiah	13
Rowley, R. C.	41
Rowell, Daniel	35
Royal, Thomas	140
Russell, Philip	175
Rutherford, Larkin	149
Ryan, James	24
Saucier, Jean Baptiste	151
Saunders, George	112
Sawine, Samuel	64
Scarborough, John	171
Scholl, Abraham	118
Scott, John	29
Scott, William	112
Scott, William	155
Scroggin, Humphrey	72
Scroggins, Jonah	49
Seagraves, Jacob	21
Sellers, Howell	119
Seybok, Robert	127
Seymour, Jarrett	112
Sharp, William	127
Shaw, Newton	16
Shaw, Samuel	10
Shepherd, Charles	10
Shipman, David	28
Shipman, David	152
Sholl, Peter	171
Short, Joshua	99
Simpkins, John G.	175
Simpson, William	167
Sims, Augustus	112
Sloan, Thomas	167
Smart, Laban	86
Smith, Aaron	49
Smith, Benjamin	36
Smith, Elijah	126
Smith, Elisha	113
Smith, Henry	126
Sommers, Stephen	163
Sornberger, George	67
Sowers, John	155
Spencer, William	71
Six (Saxe), John	14
Stamm, George	127
Steele, Capt. John	127
Stewart, Alexander	163
Stewart, William	171
Stillwell, John	163

Stiles, Richard	14	Unknown French Soldier	45
Stokes, Edmond	113	Ulmer, Jacob	41
Stopplebean, John	128	Unsell, Frederick	20
Stout, Jesse	143	Vaughn, Frederick	64
Strahan, David	11	Veath (Veach), Elias	172
Strange, John	67	Verden, James	37
Strawn, Isaiah	120	Vick, Joshua	155
Stringfield, John	140	Vincent, William	30
Stuart, James	167	Vinciner, George	50
Stufflebean, John	128	Waddell, James	140
Sturgis, Aaron	15	Wade, Obadiah	143
Summers, Joseph	143	Walker, Benjamin	99
Sutton, William	45	Walker, Henry	37
Tanner, Samuel	39	Warner, Joseph	91
Taylor, George	142	Watson, Abner	99
Taylor, Jesse	52	West, Benjamin	150
Taylor, John	29	West, Hezekiah	62
Taylor, Richard	119	West, Nathaniel	17
Tedrich, Michael	21	West, Robert	45
Teel, Levi	128	Whittaker, Alexander	128
Terry, Stephen	71	White, John	140
Thadowen, John	45	White, John	164
Tharp, Wilson	35	White, Thomas	13
Thaxton, William	49	Whitehead, Robert	128
Thomas, James	99	Whiteside, John	103
Thomas, Col. John	149	Wiggs, William	62
Thompson, Alexander	172	Willard, William	93
Thompson, James	72	Williams, Henry J.	52
Thompson, John	50	Williams, Joseph J.	58
Thompson, John	172	Williams, Isaiah	14
Thompson, Thomas	163	Williams, Thomas	60
Thornhill, Henry	86	Williamson, Jacob	97
Tipsoward, Griffin	24	Williamson, Thomas	56
Todd, Benjamin	37	Wood, Abraham	35
Toulouse, Joseph	130	Wood, Dr. Daniel	11
Toliday, John	97	Wood, John	113
Trottier, Francis	151	Wood, John	164
Turner, Andrew	113	Worth, Asa	54
Turner, Jabez	87	Wright, Capt. James	113
Turley, James	72	Wright, Joseph	103
Tuttle, Andrew	163	Yancey, Austin	41
Tutwiler, John	35	Young, Samuel	90
Tyner, Joshua	39	Zoll, Christopher	41
Underwood, Phineas	16	Zoll, Jacob	39

www.ingramcontent.com/pod-product-compliance
Lightning Source LLC
Chambersburg PA
CBHW062047220426
43662CB00010B/1689